HEALING THE MODERN BRAIN

ALSO BY DREW RAMSEY, MD

Eat to Beat Depression and Anxiety

Eat Complete

Fifty Shades of Kale

The Happiness Diet (with Tyler G. Graham)

HEALING THE MODERN BRAIN

Nine Tenets to Build Mental Fitness

and Revitalize Your Mind

DREW RAMSEY, MD

HARPER

An Imprint of HarperCollins*Publishers*

This book contains advice and information relating to health care. It should be used to supplement rather than replace the advice of your doctor or another trained health professional. If you know or suspect you have a health problem, it is recommended that you seek your physician's advice before embarking on any medical program or treatment. All efforts have been made to assure the accuracy of the information contained in this book as of the date of publication. This publisher and the author disclaim liability for any medical outcomes that may occur as a result of applying the methods suggested in this book.

FIRST EDITION

Designed by Bonni Leon-Berman

Library of Congress Cataloging-in-Publication Data has been applied for.

ISBN 978-0-06-337773-8

25 26 27 28 29 LBC 5 4 3 2 1

To my patients, past and present

Author's Note

To protect the confidentiality of our patients, mental health clinicians change details about their lives and experiences when we share their stories. This has always bothered me because it means the public never gets the real story about something pure, true, and sacred—and, far too often, real human healing gets reduced to something else.

I want to be clear about the stories in this book: they are all true. If you could decode that the doctor in the city is actually a veterinarian from the suburbs, you would find a real person, with real problems, who came to me for help.

The psychiatrist's office is such an important private space for people. They expect to engage in a therapeutic relationship that is built on nonjudgment and empathy. Confidentiality is paramount. Patients and therapists create a unique language and culture together. Can that really be shared? It's a conundrum. This is how I handled it for this book.

I did not try to listen in session with patients specifically for stories that would "work" for this book. These are tales from treatments past, filtered through my memory with the help of my notes. I hope to illustrate how the research presented can manifest in a person's life and help them build more Mental Fitness—and how Mental Fitness can bolster the progress made in the setting of mental health treatment. I changed several details like name, location, profession, and left out anything too specific. For example, I wouldn't want my therapist to write anything about his patient, the psychiatrist who is "obsessed with kale."

Hearing about people's raw, unfiltered inner worlds is essential to my work as a therapist. But I've learned, now twenty-odd years in practice, that we share more than we may think. It gives me comfort about the nature of people and the universe. It's not just red blood and neurons that we all have in common. Our stories are somehow unique and similar, too. There's true power in being together and being known.

Please receive the stories in these pages about my patients with the respect they deserve. Perhaps most importantly, know they are in this book because they showed the power of Mental Fitness and just what can be accomplished when it is attended to. I hope they inspire you as much as they have inspired me. They have filled my life with hope—and pushed me to keep working to better my own mental health.

Contents

Introduction

I had just rolled out of bed when I noticed one of my patients, Linda, had texted me several times over the course of the night. Over the past year, she had experienced a profound depression that was starting to interfere with both her work and her marriage. Even though she was reticent to take medication—many of my patients are—she had agreed to a trial run of a selective serotonin reuptake inhibitor (SSRI), Prozac. When I saw the series of messages, I worried that she was dealing with some uncomfortable side effects of the medicine—or maybe her symptoms were getting worse. It can take four to six weeks for patients to see an effect from the drug. Instead, I saw she had seen news reports of a recent meta-analysis that questioned whether or not the so-called "chemical imbalance" theory of depression—the hypothesis that a lack of serotonin was the cause, at least in part, of depressive and anxiety symptoms—had merit.

Did you see the *New York Times*?
If there's no proof that there's a chemical imbalance, why do I need an SSRI?
Is this medication even going to work? What is it actually going to do?
There have to be other options, right?

They were valid questions and she's certainly not the first person to ask them, even before this sweeping and systematic review of the evidence undertaken by a group of researchers at University College London. I wasn't surprised that their findings, which concluded there was "no consistent evidence" of an association between low serotonin levels and depression, were receiving so much attention. And with headlines like "The Study That Changes How We Treat Depression" and "With Chemical Imbalance Theory in Doubt, What's Next for Depression Care?" filling news and social media feeds across the globe, I wasn't surprised that Linda, who already had concerns about taking the medication, reached out.

Soon my inbox was also filling up with more questions—from other patients, and a few reporters, asking me what I thought it all meant. And, more importantly, whether it would change the way I continue to treat depression. I spent significant time that week discussing the matter with Linda, as well as many of my other patients.

The truth of the matter is that the idea that low levels of serotonin caused depression has been debated for decades. Every few years, someone questions the efficacy of antidepressant medications or publishes a new study that suggests it's time to toss out the biological theory of depression. Let's face it, the idea that the health of our brains—which run on a multitude of hormones, neurotransmitters, proteins, and other neurotrophic factors—comes down to the level of a single molecule is far too simple an explanation. Those of us who study mental health and the brain know that. Yet, as a practicing psychiatrist, I know that SSRIs, the gold standard for depression treatment, work in many of my patients who come to see me. They have helped to save countless lives. How do we square that fact with new evidence that serotonin isn't the biological mastermind that so many have made it out to be?

The brain is an enigmatic electrical storm made up of the proteins, fats, and vitamins you eat. Each day, as I sit with my patients, its mystery and complexity are readily apparent. It's high time the medical community, and really everyone, stopped thinking about brain health in terms of one-molecule solutions and started considering mental health conditions like depression, anxiety, attention-deficit hyperactivity disorder (ADHD), and addiction—and the patients living with them—more holistically.

Equally as important, we need to start thinking and talking about mental health beyond diagnosed disorders. Many of the patients I see often don't exactly meet the diagnostic criteria for depression, anxiety, or any other mental health disorder you will find listed in the *Diagnostic and Statistical Manual of Mental Disorders* (*DSM*). But they come to me because they are stressed-out, feeling down, overwhelmed, or having difficulty coping with a tough situation. I see more and more of these patients every year. They may not qualify for a specific mental health diagnosis, but they are still struggling. They still need help.

We need a new approach to cultivating mental health. It's more than past due. Today, more than fifty million Americans live with a mental health concern—and those are just the ones who are willing to admit it. Nearly five percent of adults reported having serious thoughts of suicide leading to 1.6 million suicide attempts in 2021. A startling twenty percent of adolescents experienced a major depressive episode within the last year. The rate of anxiety diagnoses is skyrocketing. And a shocking number of people who meet the criteria for depression, anxiety, or other psychiatric diagnoses go untreated. More and more people who have not received a medical diagnosis are admitting that, these days, they just don't feel quite right.

Even before the latest studies challenging the chemical imbalance hypothesis of depression, experienced mental health professionals understood that these kinds of incidence rates cannot be attributed to biology alone. We see that people's environments also play an important role in how they feel and how they interact with the world around them. The field of epigenetics, or the study of how our environments change how our genes are expressed, means that our DNA is not our health destiny. We have the power to make vital lifestyle changes that can quite literally change the way our bodies read genetic code, determining which genes are expressed and which are silenced. It means, even if you have a family history of mental health disorders, nothing is set in stone. You can counter any genes you have that may put you at risk.

What does this mean in practical terms? It means you can alter your habits in ways that optimize your Mental Fitness and, consequently, improve your mental health. You no longer have to look at your brain in terms of predestined wiring. You can take targeted actions in your day-to-day life to make your brain more fit and resilient, even in the face of chronic stress. That's powerful stuff.

The world is changing—and not always for the better. We've lived through a cruel pandemic, one that upended our lives in far too many ways. We are tethered to our phones and social media yet feel more isolated and disconnected than ever. We lack true community and purpose. We are experiencing dramatic deficits in nature and engagement—both things known to help our brains thrive. We are stressed to our breaking points, at work and at home. We carry far too much unprocessed trauma—and lack the ability to unburden ourselves. Our lives are filled with natural and man-made toxins, worming their way into our bodies and brains with every breath we take. And the Western diet, combined with an overly sedentary lifestyle, is robbing our brains of the vital nutrients they need to thrive. We, as a society, as a species, are at a breaking point. Pharmaceutical-only approaches are falling short—and it's time to look beyond them.

We need to start cultivating Mental Fitness. And the time to start is now.

PART I

UNDERSTANDING THE MODERN BRAIN

Theoretical physicist and self-proclaimed "futurologist" Michio Kaku once wrote, "The human brain has one hundred billion neurons, each neuron connected to ten thousand other neurons. Sitting on your shoulders is the most complicated object in the known universe."

The brain is responsible for every thought, feeling, and action. The feeling of warm sunlight on your skin. The quick blink of your eyes. The bright reds and yellows of autumn leaves, and the sound of them rustling in the wind. The words of an inspiring poem, carefully memorized. The movement of your lips as you recite it aloud. The feelings of exuberance during a joyful moment, or the despair as you experience profound loss. Added to that are sometimes overwhelming feelings of anger, fear, happiness, surprise, or stress.

Everything you and your body experience—and every action you take—is the product of the complex three-pound mass of nerves, fat, minerals, hormones, and electrical signals that is your brain.

It has taken centuries for scientists to gain even a small understanding of how this incredible organ does everything it does. In the twentieth century, Nobel Prize–winning researcher Charles Scott Sherrington was the first to publish studies demonstrating the way our brain cells communicate. He was the very first to coin the term *synapse*.

Synapses are the small spaces between neurons, the place where those cells can transmit vital messages through electric nerve impulses and the resulting release of neurotransmitter molecules. The size of a synapse is almost too small to conceptualize. It's a mere fifty nanometers. For context, that's about one hundred millionth of a meter—an incredibly tiny fraction of a human hair, which falls somewhere in the 80,000 to 100,000 nanometer range. But while synapses are infinitesimal in size, they have great power. Through these remarkable and tiny arenas, all movements, thoughts, and feelings are borne.

Let me explain. Imagine you—or rather, your brain, wants to do something as small as move your pinkie finger. Just a little crook, a small bend of the knuckles. Like all movements, reactions, and experiences, that movement starts in the brain. Your intention sends a signal to specialized motor neurons at an incredibly rapid pace. Those cells send messages to neighboring cells, which then send cells to other neurons down through the brain stem, across the nervous system, to your littlest finger. It's an incredible game of synapse telephone, where the message somehow remains intact and true—once it reaches your littlest finger, it will cause your finger to twitch. It's an amazing process. But what's even more amazing is that these synaptic signals, which act as a precisely tuned messaging system, do much more than just move our respective digits. With at least five hundred billion of these messages sent every single second, they form the basis of all human experience.

Modern neuroimaging tools mean that, for the first time, we can see the brain growing and changing. Until very recently, the field of neuroscience believed that adults could not grow new brain cells. You'd reach a certain age and—BING!—your brain was fully formed. When I was in medical school, we were taught that while all other bodily cells would continue to reproduce throughout your life, humans were gifted with only one set of brain cells: about a hundred billion or so. With luck, you'd manage not to kill off too many as you aged. Now, however, scientists have demonstrated that the brain, just like the rest of the body, continues to change and grow, well into our golden years. We experience neurogenesis, or the birth of new brain cells. We also harbor an innate ability to make new synaptic connections between cells. That's neuroplasticity.

The fact that our brains continue to evolve across our lifespan is important. It means that each of us has a degree of agency over our brain health. As we've seen more and more work from animal studies, psychological experiments, neuroimaging work, and randomized clinical trials, it's clear that our habits, lifestyle, and decisions allow us to play an important role in shaping our brains' continued growth and development. When we can make more educated decisions about what we eat, how we move, how we sleep, how we engage, who we interact with, and how we manage stress, we can modify the way our genes are expressed and support a healthy, happy brain. We can cultivate Mental Fitness.

UNDERSTANDING DEPRESSION AND ANXIETY

Terms like anxiety and depression are used in a variety of ways in everyday conversations. You hear these conditions discussed in books, movies, and your favorite television dramas. With both terms now part of the common vernacular—and the fact that both conditions are subject to stigma and misconceptions—it's not surprising that they may mean different things to different people. These days, whether you are delving into the latest scientific treatise or a wellness influencer's Instagram story, everyone has an opinion about mental health diagnoses and how to best deal with them. While the public discourse has, thankfully, grown over the last decade to shine some light on the prevalence and severity of depression and anxiety, misunderstandings about their nature still abound. And, to demonstrate why Mental Fitness is so important (more on that in a minute), it's worthwhile for us to start with some definitions.

Depression is marked by feelings of low self-worth, a down mood, sadness, lethargy, irritability, and, often, a negative bias that can make it hard for people who are suffering from it to put life's events into proper perspective. As a psychiatrist, I've met thousands of people at their lowest moment. They often describe depression as the feeling that someone turned down the dial. People in the midst of a depressive episode tend to think and speak more slowly, they look down, and they also experience anhedonia, a pernicious symptom where they can't feel joy even during happy moments. Just imagine taking a bite of your favorite food or engaging in an activity that usually thrills you but feeling, well, nothing at all. While the brain science remains a bit complicated, the clinical diagnosis of depression is pretty straightforward. The *Diagnostic and Statistical Manual of Mental Disorders* (*DSM*), the so-called bible of psychiatric diagnosis, tells us that a person has achieved a diagnosis of depression when their combination of low mood and energy starts to interfere with daily life.

Then there's anxiety. When I asked Roger McIntyre, a physician and pharmacologist at the University of Toronto who studies anxiety, to describe it for me, he said, "Anxiety is fear—fear of something, whether it's a fear of spiders or fear of social judgment."

Anxiety is the brain's reaction to a perceived threat. When you are in an anxious state, your brain sends out signals that change your physiology. Your heart and mind begin to race. Your breathing becomes fast and shallow. Your palms sweat—and your muscles tense up. You feel a sense of panic. As a result, you may experience trouble sleeping or changes in appetite.

There's a method for this anxiety madness. And it goes back to our hunter-gatherer ancestors. For them, these reactions were advantageous. They prepared the body for hypervigilance so we could avoid predators or other threats. The changes to our physiology were also helpful. They would heighten our senses—and prepare for us to fight or flee in the face of danger. It's important to understand that, thousands of years ago, a healthy anxiety response would be the difference between life and death. Fast-forward to the modern world, full of its beeps, whistles, and stressors that keep us forever on high alert, and anxiety is no longer as beneficial. Those same responses that helped us survive in the wilderness are now fueling an overactive stress response that is contributing to the incredibly high rates of anxiety disorders that we see today.

You'll notice that I often talk about depression and anxiety together. There's good reason for that. Both are debilitating mental health conditions in their own right—but they also share similar symptoms and tend to travel together. In fact, more than sixty percent of patients with a mental health diagnosis experience both anxiety and depression.

It may have caught your attention that many depressive and anxious symptoms are also part of normal human psychology. It's natural to feel anxious or sad at times. It's only when those feelings become overwhelming, or start to interfere with your work or relationships, or your ability to take care of yourself, that they have moved into a pathological place.

For years, when we've talked about depression and anxiety, we've focused on treatments—usually some form of therapy and medication. But while antidepressant and anti-anxiety medications have been game changers for many, they don't work for everyone. And, thanks to new research on lifestyle psychiatry and epigenetics, we are learning the true power of developing the tools required to handle, manage, and alleviate many of depression and anxiety's most taxing symptoms, whether you have a diagnosis or are just feeling overwhelmed by modern life.

THINKING BEYOND A "BROKEN" BRAIN

For many years, scientists and clinicians believed that DNA was the key to understanding not only our health, but our very identities. When James Watson and Francis Crick demonstrated that this incredible double-helix structure carried the genetic instructions guiding development and growth, many hoped that researchers would soon find a depression or anxiety gene that we could silence through medication or other intervention. But we are learning we are more than just a collection of genes dealt out to us before we even enter the world. Our experiences—and our choices—play an equally vital role in shaping who we are, how we think, and what we feel.

Forget the old nature versus nurture debates: the latest scientific studies have shown there is a beautiful and ongoing dance between our genes and environments. Our genes are passed down from generation to generation, providing all the data needed to create the body and mind. Certain genetic variants, often tied to different neurotransmitters or receptors, may increase or decrease our likelihood of developing a particular disease, including depression or anxiety.

For example, a mutation on the methylenetetrahydrofolate reductase gene (known as MTHFR—I'll let you sound it out for fun) has been linked to symptoms consistent with both depression and anxiety. Certainly, we've known for some time that family history matters in mental health. If one of your parents or grandparents was diagnosed with a mental health condition, it increases your likelihood of developing one. Yet, it is important to remember that genes like MTHFR are contributing, not determining, factors in disease.

My patient, Bryan, was diagnosed with depression as a teenager. He was all too familiar with the condition, having seen his mother and one of his cousins suffer through major depressive episodes. And when he came to me, he'd been taking an antidepressant medication for a number of years. The only problem was, after giving him relief initially, the SSRI was no longer working as well. He was not only suffering, but quite frustrated that his medication had stopped working for no clear reason.

Genetic testing was just becoming available and like many psychiatrists, I was excited to bring the era of genetics to my patients.

We sent Bryan's saliva sample for genetic sequencing with a promise of better understanding his illness and treatment options.

The results showed both of his MTHFR genes had mutations making them less functional. But instead of relief, he was concerned he had "the two really bad versions" of the MTHFR gene and along with his family history of depression, he was convinced his brain was somehow "broken." His particular genetic recipe meant that he'd always be living feelings of sadness and decreased motivation.

This kind of belief is not uncommon. Far too many people who have been diagnosed with depression or anxiety feel like they've been dealt a bad genetic hand. For too long, we've thought of DNA as the thing that writes our health destiny. When I was finishing medical school nearly twenty years ago, common wisdom held that our genes determined everything from intelligence to behavior. There was a pervasive notion that our genomes were solely responsible for how the body and brain grow, mature, and function—and whatever combination of genes you were born with determined, well, everything.

The good news is that notion of genetic destiny is not only outdated, but false. One of the most exciting and, frankly, empowering concepts to emerge in science in the last few decades is that of epigenetics, or the study of how environmental factors influence how our genes are expressed. As it turns out, our lifestyle decisions matter—and matter a lot. While our genes can and do predispose us for certain conditions, the choices we make day in and day out can mitigate those risks, meaning our individual DNA is much more malleable than we ever imagined. The foods we eat, the amount of sleep we get, the people we interact with, the stressors we face, and the way we move can quite literally change how our bodies read DNA sequences, influencing which genes are expressed and which are silenced.

Epigenetics is complex—and scientists are only beginning to discover all the different ways that lifestyle choices can influence genetic expression. But an easy way to conceptualize epigenetics is to think of your genome as a desktop computer. When you opened the box, all the hardware was there—much like the genome passed to you by your mother and father. But for that desktop computer to be anything but a big, clunky box, the internal hardware needs software to tell it what to do. The epigenome is like that software. Your life experiences, as well as powerful lifestyle factors like diet, exercise, social interactions, sleep, purpose, and more, can all modulate your DNA. It can determine what genetic programs are run by telling your genome to increase, decrease, or even stop production of specific proteins.

Why does this matter? Because it means that no one, no matter how stark a family medical history they may have, has a "broken" brain. No mental health conditions, or any other health conditions, are set in stone. That epigenetic software means you can make targeted changes to your lifestyle to help counter inherited genes that may increase your risk of developing a certain condition. You have the power to improve your brain health and, as a consequence, better manage depressive or anxiety symptoms.

This may be the most important thing to understand about the modern brain. Thanks to epigenetics, you can improve the expression of your genes to optimize your Mental Fitness and improve your mental health. You are much more than your genome. There is a wide variety of different things you can do to heal the modern brain, no matter what genetic profile you may be working with. So instead of looking at the brain in terms of predestined wiring, it is important to take a step back and appreciate the infinite complexity that arises from the juxtaposition of your DNA and your environment. By doing so, we can set the stage to understand the factors that influence our mental health—and build the habits we need in our daily lives to enhance the power of our modern brains.

CHAPTER 1

The Need for Mental Fitness

Experts around the globe—from the World Health Organization to the Pew Research Center—all agree: we are in the midst of a mental health epidemic. Depression and anxiety represent the two most common and disabling mental disorders in the world, with over fifty-eight million people in the United States alone affected each year.

Today, almost fourteen percent of adults in the United States take an antidepressant medication—including one in four women over the age of sixty years. Thanks to rigorous scientific research, we understand more about mental health disorders than ever before. And while access to effective treatment is improving, it would be a mistake to believe this mental health epidemic does not threaten each and every one of us.

The field of psychiatry is at a crossroads. The latest studies show that our go-to for treating conditions like depression and anxiety, SSRIs, are not the panacea we once thought they were. New research suggests that theories linking depression to serotonin deficiency remain contradictory at best, and don't account for the many other neurochemical players at work, including vital neuromolecules like glutamine, GABA, dopamine, and anandamide, just to name a few.

But the need for Mental Fitness goes beyond those with a mental health diagnosis. Today, more and more people feel overwhelmed by the demands of the modern world. They may not meet the criteria for depression or anxiety but they just don't feel *good*. Something is missing from their lives, but they can't quite figure out what it is or what to do about it. They, too, are looking for answers about how to improve their mood, better adapt to the demands of their environment, and just feel better.

It's time for a new approach: empowering lifestyle changes that promote Mental Fitness. Such changes can not only help to move the needle on the growing number of mental health diagnoses— they can also help those of us who just don't feel at our mental and physical best.

So, what is Mental Fitness, might you ask? Simply defined, it is the knowledge, patterns, habits, and skills that culminate in a more enjoyable, more mentally sound life.

Let me repeat that: Mental Fitness is the knowledge, patterns, habits, and skills that culminate in a more enjoyable, more mentally sound life.

Mental Fitness is not a result. It's a journey and a practice. It's an approach to living that takes into consideration the unrealistic demands of modern life, time, choice, genetics, lifestyle, diet, habits, chemistry, movement, rest, and mindset. Mental Fitness is a process that will help to put your brain in a perpetual state of self-repair and evolution. It will ensure your brain has the support it needs to help you weather day-to-day stress, decision fatigue, and uncertainty.

No doubt, you've read countless articles about the importance of sleep, food, physical activity, and reduced stress to sustain strong mental health. You've scanned diet and exercise blogs, maybe tried a couple of things that your favorite Instagram influencer recommended. You've heard hundreds of tips: start each day with eight ounces of celery juice and replace milk with butter in your morning cup of joe. You've read a listicle about improving your sleep hygiene and maybe even invested in a weighted blanket. There's no end to products and services that promise to make you feel better. Maybe, if you're like me, you've even tried a few. Okay, maybe more than a few. As an ever-changing world forces us to adapt to it at an increased clip, goodness knows there are more people than ever out there trying to sell you a quick fix to improve your mood, your focus, and your overall outlook on life.

The problem is, most don't work over the long haul.

It's important to understand that Mental Fitness goes beyond the concept of "wellness," or at least the version of wellness that is being marketed to you. Achieving Mental Fitness requires more than just putting down your credit card.

We are constantly being bombarded with quick fixes that will supposedly help us become the people we aspire to be. Unfortunately, while the path to Mental Fitness is pretty simple, it's not always easy. It requires foundational, yet sustainable, changes to the way you live your life day in and day out. But, as I've seen in both myself and my patients, when the focus is on building that foundation, the best results emerge.

Rather than complicate matters—let's face it, the brain is complicated enough—I want to simplify them. It's time we stopped thinking only about singular superfood and miracle products and get back to the root of good mental health. You need the foundational knowledge and tools to give you the confidence and clarity required to make the kind of choices that will make your brain more agile and resilient.

More and more, scientists are understanding that healthy brains are made, not born. Thanks to epigenetics, we understand that our habits and decisions hold a lot of sway over both our mental and physical health. We also understand that by viewing mental health only through the lens of a diagnosis, we are doing a huge disservice to all. To become happier and healthier, we could all benefit from working on feeling better, regardless of whether we've been given a specific diagnosis. By adopting habits that facilitate Mental Fitness, you can take control of your own mental health. That's powerful stuff.

CHAPTER 2

Obstacles to Mental Fitness

I've been practicing psychiatry for over twenty years and I can't help but notice significant changes in my patients from when I started my career. The modern world is taking its toll on the human brain. Our daily lives are set up to all but guarantee we feel distracted and overwhelmed. We are tethered to the smart devices of our choice, constantly bombarding us with alerts, while we let our personal relationships languish. We consume overprocessed foods that lack the healthy nutrients so vital to nourishing our bodies and brains. We face unrelenting financial pressures, and are receiving near-constant messages about violence and disasters around the globe. Let's face it, today's environment is simply not conducive to brain health.

Is it any wonder that so many of us are struggling with our mental health?

PROTECTING YOUR BRAIN

The world has changed a lot in the past few decades and, too often, it has not been to our benefit. Luckily, our understanding of the human brain has changed, too. We now know that we achieve optimal brain health when we cultivate the big three brain protectants: increased neuroplasticity, decreased inflammation, and a more diverse microbiome.

It's likely you've heard these terms before. Neuroplasticity has gotten a lot of ink in recent years—especially since it has changed the way we think about brain-related illness. Once upon a time, most scientists believed that you were born with a set of about one hundred billion brain cells and that was that. If you were clinically depressed, without the help of strong medicine, years of psychoanalysis, or electroshock therapy, you were probably going to stay that way. Now, however, we understand that that couldn't be further from the truth. The brain, much like the rest of your body, has the ability to change and grow as we age. That's a good thing. That means that you are not doomed to stay in whatever state you may find yourself in now—especially if it is a depressed or anxious one. When you cultivate Mental Fitness, you can help your brain stay in "grow mode," and make it more resilient in the face of the world's stressors.

While you increase neuroplasticity, you need to simultaneously reduce inflammation. Many of the foods we eat and toxins we encounter can lead to brain inflammation. Normally, inflammation is a good thing. It's a sign that your immune system is working, protecting you from viral or bacterial invaders, or providing your organs the molecules they need to repair cells after injury. But, as with anything else, you can have too much of a good thing. The latest studies show us that persistent, chronic inflammation is a serious problem. And when you find it in the brain, it can lead to depressive and anxiety symptoms, as well as sleep problems. Working toward Mental Fitness can help deal with excess inflammation.

Scientists have also demonstrated the importance of a healthy gut to mental health. I realize it may seem somewhat confusing. What does your gastrointestinal tract have to do with your brain, after all? As it turns out, quite a bit. The colonies of bacteria that live in our guts do far more than just digest the food that we eat so we can take the energy we need from it. They also act as chemical messengers, providing the brain with key updates about the world around us. When we have a healthy gut, full of the right populations of bacteria, or "good bugs," we know that our brain is receiving all the right messages—and, as a result, is more resilient in the face of stress and other factors that can lead to depression or anxiety. Again, here, the habits that can increase your Mental Fitness can also keep your gut health in check.

In the following chapters, we're going to talk a lot about the practical, everyday things you can do to promote neuroplasticity and a diverse microbiome, while keeping excess inflammation to a minimum. But I think it is also important to highlight some of the top obstacles to achieving Mental Fitness—and how these seemingly small things can have quite a big impact on our brains, especially over time. Many of these obstacles seem almost ubiquitous in the modern world—which is why it's so important to call them out. Some of them you've likely already read about, but a few may surprise you.

Devices

Today, nearly everyone carries around a small, magical device in their pocket. Smartphones and other smart devices are amazing. They grant you access to incredible knowledge and have the power to connect you to people all over the world. But for all their benefits, they can interfere with Mental Fitness. The artificial light from their screens can wreak havoc on our bodies' circadian rhythms. The fast-paced content, as well as all of the notifications and alarms built into different apps, is specifically designed to pull your attention in a hundred different directions. It can put us into a state of sensory overload, which releases cortisol and puts us into a stress state. And I would be remiss if I didn't mention that a lot of the content we gravitate toward isn't the best for us. Far too often, we "doomscroll" across disturbing news or content—or just zone out—when our mental health would be better served by putting down our phones and engaging in other activities.

Vices and Substances

The human brain loves a good shortcut. That's why human beings are hardwired to pick up habits. They allow the brain to let some processes roll out automatically—so it doesn't have to consciously oversee *everything*. There's nothing wrong with habits per se. But many of our automatic, go-to behaviors involve substances. Think about it. We wake up, get coffee into us as soon as we can. If we have a stressful day, we may smoke—or vape. We come home and grab a drink to help us wind down after a tough day.

As a society, our relationship with vices is complicated—especially as most of these substances are not only legal, but actively promoted as ways to help enjoy life (and maybe deal with your day-to-day stress along the way). But what are these substances doing to our brains, exactly?

Thanks to public health campaigns, we now understand that caffeine, nicotine, alcohol, and marijuana can act as a sort of false neurotransmitter, increasing or decreasing brain activity while triggering pleasurable, calming sensations. There's a reason why we reach for a beer or light up a cigarette—they are incredibly effective in reducing stressful feelings, at least temporarily.

Unfortunately, while the cardiovascular and general health risks of substances like alcohol and tobacco are widely discussed, as well as the risks of addiction, their influence on brain health tends to be ignored. And the latest studies show us that both drinking and smoking are heavily linked to increases in brain inflammation. Which, as we discussed above, is strongly associated with depression, anxiety, and neurodegeneration.

Pollutants and Toxins

At the cellular level, an entire world of environmental toxins is attacking the cells in both our bodies and brains. But while the media (particularly social media) abounds with stories about poisons in the modern world, whether or not a substance is dangerous often depends on the dose. As you think about brain health, it's important to understand what is really toxic to your brain.

Dorland's Medical Dictionary defines toxin as "a poison, especially a protein or conjugated protein produced by certain animals, higher plants, and pathogenic bacteria." That definition is a bit outdated. Dorland didn't consider man-made toxins—and, in today's world, there are plenty of synthetic molecules that can cause inflammation, depression, and anxiety. Unfortunately, thanks to modern industry, there are more harmful substances in the environment than there have ever been before in human history.

For example, you may have heard of phthalates, chemicals found in just about every plastic product known to man. These molecules have come under deep scrutiny in recent years because of laboratory studies that show they can disrupt endocrine function. Simply defined, they can interfere with the body's hormonal systems, which, of course, play a vital role in brain function.

Heavy metals like mercury, cadmium, and lead are increasing in the water—and affecting our food supply. There are pesticides, xenoestrogens, and all manner of other chemicals in the food system, too.

Studies suggest that women, on average, consume 168 chemicals each and every day through self-care products like skin creams, shampoos, and makeup. Today's foods contain untold numbers of artificial chemicals, dyes, flavorings, preservatives, and fillers.

Unfortunately, there is not a ton of research on the relationships between environmental toxicity and inflammation—but what there is suggests that lower-level toxic exposures may accumulate over time, increasing inflammation and promoting cellular degeneration. That means our brains are vulnerable to environmental toxins—and it's likely that they play a role in the rising rates of depression and anxiety.

Ultraprocessed Foods

We are going to talk about diet in detail in Chapter 4—but I should mention that the modern Western diet, increasingly based on ultraprocessed foods, is another obstacle to our brains working their best. High-calorie convenience foods lack the nutrients our brains need to thrive. They disrupt brain growth and contribute to excess inflammation. And they are getting in the way of our ability to cultivate Mental Fitness.

Chronic Stress

We are all familiar with the feeling of stress: the clenching in your chest, the tension across your temples, the racing of the mind. You may have experienced it when running to meet an important deadline—or when arguing with someone you love.

Stress is a universal experience—and it's one designed to keep us alive. Back in our hunter-gatherer days, as we searched for food while evading predators, the brain would put us into a stress mode to help keep us alert and equip us to deal with any potential danger with efficiency. But stress was never meant to be a chronic condition. The brain was simply supposed to release stress hormones like cortisol to help you more effectively fight, flee, freeze, or fawn to dodge a dangerous situation and then bring you back down to baseline.

Unfortunately, for millions of people in the modern world, stress is a constant. In 2020, two out of three adults reported they felt increased stress as compared to the previous year. And the physiological changes that stress brings, over the long term, can result in increased inflammation, lowered neurotrophic factor production (you can think of these molecules as "brain fertilizer" to help keep your brain in grow mode), and less-than-diverse microbiomes. All things we should avoid. People with chronic stress also report fatigue and insomnia. And, as we discussed above, it can drive us to less-than-optimal habits like drinking and smoking.

Given that the majority of diagnosed cases of clinical anxiety and depression involve heightened stress, it's important to acknowledge that our busy, modern worlds are contributing to mental health issues. We are asking too much of ourselves, and it's taking a toll on our brain health.

Certainly, this is not an exhaustive list of obstacles to Mental Fitness. I could go on—but the majority of issues we face in the modern world link back to these five broad categories. They interact with one another and, ultimately, come together in different ways to interfere with us doing what we need to do to heal our brains.

These obstacles, of course, aren't going away anytime soon. And they don't necessarily need to. But we need to be conscious of what role they play in our lives—and what impact they may have on our brain health. Knowledge is power. It can help you determine which of these may be getting in the way of your own Mental Fitness practices.

I hope it will become clear to you in this book that healing the modern brain isn't about running marathons—physical or emotional—or having to give up all the things you love to eat. It's not about competition or embracing a life of scarcity. It's not even about ridding yourselves of all the obstacles we just talked about above.

It's about adopting Mental Fitness practices. Simply stated, Mental Fitness is a radical and personal form of self-care. And it's an approach that each person can design around her or his own culture, needs, and preferences. It's not an all-or-nothing approach. Rather, it's a series of small changes that can lead to big results.

As you read the following pages, you'll soon see there's no need to hang on to one-molecule solutions to depression or anxiety—or even wait for our mental health to decline enough to receive a diagnosis. Instead, each and every one of us has the power to make more educated decisions about what we eat, how we move, how we sleep, and how we manage stress in order to optimize our Mental Fitness. These small changes have the power to beget larger ones, as the core tenets build upon each other, ultimately creating an outpouring of benefits that help build resilience and protect our brains from the modern world.

Are you ready to start?

PART II

THE CORE TENETS OF MENTAL FITNESS

With a basic understanding of how the brain works—as well as the obstacles that are keeping it from achieving optimal health—we can now talk about the foundational building blocks that promote Mental Fitness.

As I noted before, neuroplasticity, inflammation, and the microbiome all play key roles in our overall health. Unfortunately, the modern world is filled with variables that dampen our brain's capacity for growth, promote inflammation, and kill the good bugs in your gut. But when you embrace the core tenets of Mental Fitness, you can counteract these negative forces. You can ensure that your brain stays in grow mode, even during stressful times. You can promote the growth of beneficial bacteria throughout the gastrointestinal tract, helping to facilitate those vital gut-brain messages that keep the whole body healthy. And you can keep inflammation in check—giving your immune system the signals it needs so it does not overreact and send hordes of inflammatory molecules into the brain. Truly, when you adopt a Mental Fitness approach, choosing healthy habits that promote brain health, you can teach your brain to be more resilient. That's what we all need.

So, let's talk about these core tenets of remarkable brain goodness. I've already mentioned several of them, including nutrition, sleep, and connection. But in the following chapters, I'll take a deep dive into the following subjects, explaining why each is so important to brain health—and what steps you can take to leverage that knowledge to get your brain into fighting shape.

The Core Tenets of Mental Fitness are:

1. *Self-awareness:* I know, I know—everyone is talking about mindfulness these days. But you don't have to be a yogi or a Buddhist monk to enjoy a boost from moments of introspection. When you develop an awareness of your body, breath, and mood, you will find you are in a stronger position to handle whatever the world throws your way.
2. *Nutrition:* How you fuel your body and brain is important. When you learn how to best nourish your brain—and yourself—you are taking the first step on the path to Mental Fitness.
3. *Movement:* The brain may not be a muscle, but it was designed to thrive in response to a healthy, moving body. Few things can promote brain growth and protect your mental health as powerfully as movement.
4. *Sleep:* For a long time, we've thought of sleep as a time of rest. We now understand the brain is hard at work, clearing out debris and consolidating memories while we slumber. A good night's sleep is a cornerstone of Mental Fitness.
5. *Connection*: Connection is a fundamental piece of feeling your best mentally and emotionally. Connecting to yourself, your purpose, the people around you—these are all ways to promote Mental Fitness.
6. *Engagement:* There is a great advantage to keeping an actively engaged mind. Activities that stretch your intellectual capabilities a bit can fuel both creativity and cognitive flexibility. This helps the brain stay in shape as we grow older.
7. *Grounding:* In this day and age, it's easy to forget that our brains weren't designed to engage in a fully digital world. The brain thrives when we get out into green and open spaces—and it's something that many of us have forgotten and desperately need.

8. *Unburdening:* There's no two ways about it, we can't keep swallowing our trauma and expect to remain physically or mentally healthy. It's time to find ways to process our past experiences so we can move forward, as well as develop the kinds of habits that will keep us mentally fit despite our past experiences.

9. *Purpose:* Identifying and working toward our goals, big and small, can have a huge impact on not only our self-esteem, but our resilience in the face of stress. Learn to protect your time and pursue your true purpose.

By making small, consistent lifestyle changes, you can have tremendous impact on your mental health and well-being. You are in the driver's seat—making the decisions that can amp up neurogenesis, fight inflammation, and increase the diversity in your microbiome. Each tenet builds upon the next, working together to improve your Mental Fitness and optimize your mental health. This is a case where the whole is truly more than the sum of its parts. And, best of all, you can do it your way.

Let's get to it.

CHAPTER 3

Self-Awareness

Charlotte had never been a big drinker. During her college years, she was the friend who made do with half a beer (or all-out abstained) in order to make sure her friends made it home safely. Before she married, when she was working as an editorial assistant for a magazine, she might occasionally have a glass of wine at work parties or when she went out with friends. For the most part, she told me, she could really take it or leave it.

Now married with three kids, Charlotte would sometimes accept a glass of red wine if her husband offered her one once they put the kids down for the night. And, she admitted, she might "go big" with a second glass on those rare occasions when she and her husband managed to sneak in a night out on their own and ordered a bottle of something special. But alcohol had never been a big draw for her. She didn't feel its pull the way that so many other people seemed to.

And then the COVID-19 pandemic happened.

Wrangling her three kids 24/7—including all the extra duties that came with virtual schooling—took its toll. She thought she knew how to juggle things as a busy stay-at-home mom. But the pandemic required so much more of her, and she felt the stress of those first few months of lockdown keenly. Each day, Charlotte exhausted herself as she tried to keep the kids engaged with online lessons and other activities (and away from the former game room, which had been taken over by her husband as a makeshift office). Between trying to manage all the unknowns surrounding this new virus—and three bored and hyperactive kids between the ages of five and twelve—she was frazzled. It didn't help that her normal stress relievers, which included weekly dance classes and regular outings with friends, were no longer available to her.

Her one and only break came each day around six o'clock in the evening, when her husband ended his last conference call and entertained the kids while she made dinner. Charlotte said she's not sure exactly when it started, but she began pouring herself a glass of wine each night as she put the meal together. Her husband may have even suggested it. The glass was just supposed to be a little something to help her relax.

Over time, that one glass became two. Two became three. By the time lockdown ended and the kids were back in school, Charlotte realized she was drinking *at least* a bottle of wine each night. She was shocked by how much alcohol she had been consuming—and continued to consume without a second thought. It was affecting her sleep. It was affecting her mood. Yet, she couldn't quite figure out how to lessen or stop her intake. That's when she came to see me.

"I didn't even realize what was happening," she told me. "I've never been a drinker. Now, all of a sudden, I am? And even if I needed a little something to help during lockdown, that's over now. But even when I tell myself I'm not going to have a glass, come dinnertime, it's like I'm on some kind of wine-pouring autopilot. I don't even realize that I have a glass in my hand until it's almost empty."

THE POWER OF SELF-AWARENESS

It's often said that you can't manage what you can't measure. But I would say, before you start thinking about any sort of metrics, you must first be aware there is an issue that you need to address. Because there is no way you can manage what you might not even notice. Sigmund Freud, founder of psychoanalysis, was fond of saying that the goal of psychoanalytic work was to "make the unconscious conscious." It's the main goal of what we psychiatrists do in psychotherapy with our patients. Until we see ourselves—and our coping mechanisms—clearly, it's nearly impossible to find healthier ways of navigating the world around us. That's why self-awareness really is a keystone of Mental Fitness. Far too many of us walk around this world without paying heed to our habits—what triggers them, what supports them, and what solace they bring us. For Charlotte, that lack of self-awareness led to her drinking more wine than she wanted to. For others, it may involve staying up too late scrolling Instagram, interfering with a good night's rest. Still others may binge on junk food while zoning out to a television show or find themselves unconsciously avoiding social obligations. It's all too easy to say that this is simply a lack of self-discipline—but these kinds of less-than-ideal coping skills spring up when we stay oblivious to our feelings, our needs, and the best way to manage them.

There are many things we each can do to help cultivate Mental Fitness. But until we become more self-aware—taking notice of the patterns and behaviors that may be interfering with healing the modern brain—it is impossible to make the necessary changes to get there. It all starts, to steal Freud's line, by making the "unconscious conscious." No therapy required.

These days, there's a lot of talk about "mindfulness"—one of the clear signs we are paying more attention to our mental health. But often there isn't as much discussion about what exactly mindfulness should look like. I've met many patients over the years who grimace at the idea. They tell me, "I've tried that. Doesn't work for me." When you hear the word, you may immediately think of monks or meditation retreats. That friend or family member who is always recommending a particular yoga class or relaxation app may also come to mind. While those things can help some people get to a more mindful state, they aren't essential. For our purposes, it's important to go back to the basics of what mindfulness is—and that's being self-aware. Mindfulness is simply finding a way to be fully present in the moment, while developing the ability to know where you are, what you are doing, and how you are feeling. This is what will allow you to assess, even at the most basic level, your habits, your needs, and your overall well-being. Self-awareness is key to you making change.

It is the foundation of Mental Fitness. And, sadly, most of us aren't very good at it.

In the classic 1980s movie *Bull Durham*, Annie Savoy, played by Susan Sarandon, quips, "The world is made for people who aren't cursed with self-awareness." She's right. Western culture promotes busyness and convenience. We are supposed to be constantly active and productive. We juggle, multitask, and still are left feeling like we haven't done enough. There's no time for self-reflection when we are expected to just keep moving without considering what it's doing to our bodies and brains. Our calendars are overly full, and we often describe ourselves as "too busy."

Then there's social media's take on self-awareness. While there has been amazing scientific work providing evidence that mindfulness has significant benefits for the human brain, it's been co-opted by those trying to sell you something, usually promising that a product, app, or subscription service will make it easier to be mindful. But you don't need to meditate for hours on end to build self-awareness. It's not necessary to take a class or download an app that boasts a fellow with a soothing English accent reminding you to be grateful. A few of my patients have gotten help from these, but not for long. Believe it or not, you already have all the tools you need to become more self-aware. And that begins with you slowing down and taking a more observational approach to your life.

At our first appointment, Charlotte confessed her worry that she would be unable to stop drinking. Yet, she had already taken a pivotal first step to foment change: she observed that she had developed a habit that was not serving her or her mental health. When you become more self-aware, you put yourself in a position of true power. You can take a step back and look at the different ways your environment, your relationships, and your own inner critic may be pushing you to work against your own brain health. But most importantly, once you do take notice of these different variables, you can put the right road map in place to better manage them. You can give yourself the power to take charge of your own Mental Fitness.

UNDERSTANDING HABITS

Before we talk about how to move into a more observational mode, it's probably worthwhile to do a quick primer on how human beings develop habits, or specific behaviors that have become routine. The brain is designed to help you build habits. Think about it: the human brain has a lot on its plate. It's in charge of every thought, every feeling, and every movement. It is charged with not only all the autonomic functions that keep you alive, but all the other stuff that allows you to freely navigate the world around you.

Because it's such a busy organ, it does not have the bandwidth to handle everything at a conscious level. Consider breathing. Imagine if you had to consciously tell your brain to tell your lungs to pull in some of that sweet, sweet oxygen on the regular. You wouldn't be able to concentrate on anything else. Your brain, however, makes sure breathing doesn't take up too many resources by making it automatic. You don't have to think about breathing to inhale the oxygen you need. It just happens unconsciously—so your brain can concentrate on all the other things it needs to do.

While breathing isn't exactly a habit per se, it is something that doesn't require conscious maintenance. As we grow, learn, and pick up other skills beyond the basic bodily necessities, we want—no, need—to make sure they aren't too taxing on the brain. We want to make them unconscious. So, for the most part, any regular behavior that becomes second nature—that you engage in without conscious thought—is a type of habit. When we hear the alarm clock in the morning, we automatically shuffle into the kitchen, often with our eyes still half-closed, to start the coffeemaker. You receive a tense work email, and you unconsciously start to bite your fingernails. Once you close the car door, you immediately put on your seat belt. You head to the movie theater to see the latest blockbuster and head straight to the concession line even if you aren't truly hungry. When we see the big deadline on our calendar, we procrastinate instead of getting right down to work. Or, if you are like Charlotte, when you start making dinner, you reflexively pour a glass of wine.

Your brain is always on the lookout for rewards—whether it be food, drink, love, or just a little stress release. When you engage in a behavior that leads to a reward, the brain takes notice. It will dole out a hit of a special neurotransmitter, dopamine, in response.

It's likely you've heard about dopamine before. Many call it the brain's "pleasure" chemical. But it's much more than that. It's actually a learning chemical. It's there to tell us what's good—so we know to continue going after it. The latest neuroscience studies tell us that dopamine is released *before* we complete a certain task or behavior, so we continue to seek out a particular reward or take action to avoid something threatening or stressful. Dopamine can act as both a carrot and a stick—but it's there to motivate us toward action. It's also there to help us develop all those brain-resource-saving habits.

As you repeat actions over time, your brain will build new neural pathways that will eventually form habit loops. The dopamine you receive as part of your behavior will help you make a particular behavior part of your routine. The more often you do it, the less you have to think about it—and a habit is born.

Research studies suggest it can take anywhere from 18 to 254 days to solidify a single habit, whether it's drinking a glass of water every morning, brushing your teeth before bed, taking a daily run, or any other regular behavior. Time and repetition make rit-ual, hardwiring certain actions directly into your brain to the point where they becomes second nature.

It's helpful to understand the habit loop in three parts: cue, rou-tine, and reward. Let's consider Charlotte's wine-drinking habit. The cue is dinnertime—that first break where she has a few min-utes where she isn't responsible for everyone else. The routine is pouring the glass of wine. At first it was a one-off but, over time, it became part of her dinnertime routine. She would pour the glass without even thinking about it. Finally, there is the reward. The alcohol, which is a depressant, slows down the central nervous system, temporarily giving feelings of relaxation. Alcohol also hap-pens to stimulate the opioid receptor, a type of receptor that can result in a feeling mild euphoria, which also adds to those good feelings. But alcohol is not the only reward in this scenario. Other factors also played a role in building this habit. The reward of hav-ing that time to herself after a busy day. The reward of knowing her children are being well cared for by their father. The reward of the good meal to come. All of these different things came together to help Charlotte build this habit. And they should all be considered now that she's decided she needs to break it.

Now that you understand how habits are formed—and what is required to break them—you can see why self-awareness plays such an important role in cultivating Mental Fitness.

IF YOU MAKE IT, YOU CAN BREAK IT

Habits can become deeply ingrained. But that does not mean they are unbreakable. If you have developed a habit that is no longer serving you, like Charlotte had with her nighttime wine drinking, you can rid yourself of it. And that starts with self-awareness. Once you recognize the habit you want to break, you need to figure out how to remove or at least be more cognizant of the cues that prompt you to engage in it, wherever possible, and replace any reward you may obtain from it.

In Charlotte's case, she needed something to help her wind down in the evening as she prepared dinner. Instead of pouring a glass of wine, we discussed different replacement options. Might she want a fun mocktail? A glass of pomegranate juice with a little bit of sparkling water in a wineglass? Or my go-to—a little kombucha? The idea was to have a drink she enjoyed to replace the wine. Something that added a little bit of a relaxing ritual to dinner prep, without the alcohol.

Another patient of mine, Andy, had a terrible nail-biting habit. He was someone who took great pride in his appearance, always dressing in the latest fashions. He was always perfectly put together. Until you looked at his nails.

"My anxiety takes my fingers straight into my mouth," he said. "I don't even realize I'm doing it."

He had tried everything—keeping his nails supershort, using a bitter-tasting nail polish, and even, at his lowest point, hypnosis. Nothing, so far, had worked for him. I asked him to take a step back and try to make himself more aware of when he was biting his nails. Write down some of his triggers. Like Charlotte, he quickly saw some common patterns—usually involving work issues.

Once Andy was more aware of what would usually lead him to chew his nails, it was time to consider a replacement activity. He was skeptical when I suggested that he buy a fancy manicure kit. He literally laughed out loud. But for someone who took as many pains with his appearance, I thought it was a great idea. When he felt the stress that usually led him to chew his nails, he could replace that behavior with trimming his cuticles or buffing his nails. Within a few months, he had gorgeous fingernails—and a healthier way to deal with the stress that usually culminated in nail-biting.

I realize I'm giving you only the basics here. The point I want to emphasize is that, one, habits can be broken, and, two, doing so starts with self-awareness. That is what provides you with the ability to identify the cues that trigger your habit, as well as the meaningful replacement items or behaviors that can scratch your habit itch.

HOW TO BECOME MORE SELF-AWARE

Now, of course, you are probably asking yourself, "But how do I become more self-aware?" It's a good question.

Research studies have shown that self-awareness, or the ability to consciously monitor our inner thoughts and external behaviors, provides a host of benefits. Being able to see ourselves clearly increases confidence and creativity. It helps us make more informed decisions. It makes us better friends, lovers, and family members. We must foster self-awareness because it is a catalyst to change. And it helps us shape our Mental Fitness.

Unfortunately, becoming more self-aware doesn't always come naturally. Since the brain is designed to pick up all these habits and routines to reduce cognitive load, it does take conscious effort to look at your interactions both inside your head and in the outside world.

So how, exactly, does one start to take notice of things we do unconsciously? It starts with taking that observational stance. Pretend you are a historian or anthropologist trying to understand a particular behavior without judgment. Then take a step back and really look at whatever aspect of your life that you think may be impeding your Mental Fitness. But remember to be kind to yourself—this isn't about beating yourself up for any particular habit. This is about recognizing the situations and circumstances that may be contributing to that behavior. Think about how you would advise a dear friend in your situation to promote more positive self-talk.

Increasing and maintaining lifelong self-awareness is key—but a quick warning. Awareness itself doesn't change things. In fact, self-awareness can increase our pain at first. We become aware of the ways we are contributing to our problems or the seemingly unchangeable parameters of our situation or ourselves. Awareness takes bravery and that can be hard to muster when we are struggling. While we all can be avoidant to some degree, it helps to see that by being avoidant we actually create a cascade of bigger problems even if at first it seems easier. Facing our challenges is more difficult on the surface, but it's the only path to Mental Fitness.

Some people can easily just take a step back and observe themselves. But others can struggle. That's why I often recommend journaling as you look to increase your self-awareness. It's a great way to take stock of where you are—and where you want to be. It is a place for doodles and BIG IDEAS you write in all caps. It's a simple tool for keeping track of your habits and, ultimately, your goals. It can help you better understand the various factors that may be contributing to a particular behavior. And, perhaps just as importantly, help you figure out how to better manage it in the future.

SELF-AWARENESS JOURNALING PROMPTS

Self-awareness, at its most basic, is an act of self-discovery. Some people are adept at just writing freely about how they feel—but some people need to be prompted. Here are a few questions that can help you better journal about what you may be experiencing in the moment. The list is not meant to be exhaustive. Rather, it is to help you think about who you are, what you want, and how you feel.

Right now, I feel _____.

I wish people understood that _____ stresses me out.

The things I do best are _____.

My biggest fear is _____.

One habit I hope to build is _____.

The emotion I feel the most is _____.

I don't always feel like I can show my emotions to others. I feel like I have to hide my feelings when I _____
_____.

My mood is instantly disrupted when _____
_____.

My greatest strength is _____.

The emotions I find hardest to accept are _____
_____.

What do I do for self-care? _____.

Which emotions do I tend to avoid or push down? _____
_____.

What's going well in my life right now? _____
_____.

What is my worst habit? _____
_____.

For example, to help Charlotte become more aware of her drinking, I asked her to keep a journal in the kitchen and take a daily tally of every glass of wine she poured *before* she drank it and just a few words about how she was feeling. By keeping that running total, she could no longer unconsciously make her way through a bottle of wine. And she could see the obvious pattern—whether she was feeling stressed, annoyed, "over it," or just thirsty. Just by adding a simple tick for a new glass and her feelings on paper, she was immediately aware of how much she was drinking and any emotions she might be self-medicating.

"I'd go to put that checkmark in the journal and stop to think about how I was feeling. Even though it doesn't take all that much time to write something, it's enough time. It makes me pause and think about whether I really want another glass of wine," she said. "More often than not, I realized I really didn't. That's when I realized I needed to start writing not just before I drank, but before I even poured."

Within just a couple of weeks, Charlotte saw a significant decrease in how much wine she consumed each night.

That's one of the benefits of writing things down. It not only helps you observe what you are doing and how you are feeling in a given moment, but it also provides a little pause so you can think about what you want. It makes these unconscious habits conscious—and puts you in a position where you can think about whether you want to continue a behavior. In addition, it gives you an opportunity to consider whether there may be a different way to deal with your feelings. After Charlotte noticed a pattern of feeling irritated over several days, she continued to write in her journal to try to get to the bottom of what was amplifying that feeling for her—and how she could better manage it.

"The kids were at this stage where at least one of them hated what I was cooking. And, you know, these dishes were fan favorites before," she said. "And they would whine and complain after I made all this food, and my husband wasn't really saying anything about it. I realized that I needed him to step up and tell them to quit it."

In the past, she said, those feelings might have stayed bottled up for a while, only to come out during an argument. But by recognizing that irritation before it grew into an uncontainable mess, she was able to have a calm discussion about the matter with her husband. The next time one of the kids complained, he handled it like a pro. She said even her youngest ate all of his broccoli that evening.

"Writing things down is helping me realize how often I used to just swallow these little things until they grew and grew and just became huge for me," she said. "They really are much easier to deal with when they stay little."

I should also mention that journaling can be of benefit even if there isn't a specific behavior you are trying to manage. You can think more generally—and take pen in hand to write down your goals as well as how to best accomplish them. In doing so, you can also identify any obstacles that may be hindering your progress— and how to overcome them. It's the kind of thing that most of us do at work all the time, through planning, meetings, and emails. If we'd do it for our jobs, why wouldn't we take the time to do it for our mental health? Most importantly, what needs to change for you to take this time?

You can also use your journal to practice gratitude or reflect. Make a list of all the good things in your life. It will help you appreciate them more by—you guessed it—making you more aware of them. Take some time to write the values that are most important to you, the principles you believe are most important in guiding your life and work. Again, by putting pen to paper, you can be more aware of where you are living up to your values, as well as identify areas where you could potentially make some changes to live more in alignment with them. These exercises are also good for the brain. Sometimes we don't know what is hidden up there in our complicated emotions . . . until we write it down.

FOCUS ON THE WHAT

You can also journal about your feelings. I think this is a powerful way to exorcise some of those inner demons that can interfere with robust mental health. But too often, we use our journals as nothing more than dumping grounds for our negative emotions. While this can feel good in the moment, it may not provide the kind of insights that will help us improve our self-awareness. Research from Tasha Eurich, PhD, an organizational psychologist who studies self-awareness, suggests you can bolster your self-awareness when you focus on the *what* instead of the *why*. Her research shows that reframing the questions you ask yourself can provide actionable information to help you make changes.

Think about it. Far too often, our introspection is nothing more than why. Why did I say that? Why can't I get over this breakup? Why can't I go to bed at a reasonable hour? Why? Why? Why? Unfortunately, when we pose this question to ourselves, we tend to focus on the negatives. I said that because I was angry. I can't let go of this breakup because I'm never going to meet anyone as good as my last partner. I can't go to bed at a reasonable hour because I'm so stressed-out at work. None of those answers give you much more than continued gloomy feelings. But when you start to ask yourself *what* questions, you can think beyond the bad stuff and start thinking about potential solutions to whatever may be ailing you.

Consider the bedtime question. Instead of asking yourself why, think about *what* may be happening each night that is keeping you from catching that much-needed shut-eye. Sure, work may be seriously stressing you out right now. But focusing on that does not help you address the matter at hand: your sleep hygiene.

When you start to imagine what's happening in your personal world each night, you can better identify what may be ailing you. Many people climb in bed and immediately start doomscrolling on social media, or mindlessly accept Netflix's invitation to watch the next episode. If that's your what, putting a hard stop on screen time an hour before bed might help. Maybe you aren't struggling with screen time but tend to head to the kitchen a couple of hours after dinner to indulge in a sugary snack. As you think about that what, you may realize that nighttime eating often makes you feel too full and uncomfortable to sleep. Maybe it's time to work on removing that munching time from your nightly routine. Or it could be your what is happening even earlier. That caffeinated soda or after-dinner coffee that keeps your mind buzzing when it's time for you to shut down.

When you focus on the what, instead of the why, you'll find that you are more open to learning new information about your habits—and finding ways to manage them. You can use this approach to look at your habits, your knee-jerk reactions to particular situations (what is it about visits to my sister's house that always rubs me the wrong way?), or other things in your life that may need a light shined upon them. And then, with the insights you gain, you can determine what, if anything, you can or should do to bring yourself more peace and well-being.

NO MEDITATION TRAINING REQUIRED

Not everyone is into journaling—I understand. But every single one of us can breathe.

There's a reason why meditation is such a hot topic in the wellness space. It can help induce a heightened state of awareness in people, helping them focus their attention on the present. It can also act as a serious stress reliever, with studies showing it can reduce inflammation and help manage anxiety symptoms, which is why some of my colleagues will prescribe meditation right along with antidepressant medications.

Research studies examining the brains of Tibetan monks, who make a career out of meditating hours and hours each day, show brain activity that supports both relaxation and self-regulation—which has led researchers like Bin He, a neuroscientist at Carnegie Mellon University, to suggest that meditative practices "optimize" how the brain uses its resources, focusing attention on what's most important. He also hypothesizes that the changes observed in brain networks during meditation help bring the brain into a state of heightened neuroplasticity.

This is a good thing. We know that grow mode is a key part of

Mental Fitness. But what if you don't have time to dedicate a few hours each day to meditation? What if, like many of my patients have told me, you can't even figure out if you are actually meditating when you try to do it?

You can breathe.

Seriously, you don't need a full-blown, three-hour meditation to achieve big brain benefits (unless you want to, that is). You can get many of the same effects by just taking some time to sit and breathe.

When I was growing up, many parenting books suggested that moms and dads tell their kids to "breathe and count to ten" when they were in a heightened emotional state. This could stop them from needlessly lashing out. As it turns out, there is some science behind that advice. Taking a beat and breathing your way through a short countdown can help you better regulate your emotions—and help you consider whether you really want to say harsh words or commit to a particular action when you are upset. Believe it or not, this old chestnut is a gateway to meditation. By pausing and breathing, you can be more aware of your feelings in the moment and how they may be affecting you.

Another powerful, and I would argue, essential tool for Mental Fitness is breathwork—which takes breathing to the next level, especially for people who struggle with anxiety. At its most basic, breathwork is consciously controlling each part of the breath. Inhale for a few counts, hold for another few counts, and then deeply exhale. Repeat for two to five minutes to help calm anxiety symptoms or help bring yourself to a state of heightened awareness. While there are more complex and ancient breathing practices to explore, such as Pranayama Yoga, one thing I like about breathwork is that it is an easy practice to start. You can go with the most basic options and still feel the effects quite quickly.

In a recent randomized controlled trial, researchers at Stanford University compared the different types of breathwork to mindfulness meditation to see whether they had similar effects in terms of stress reduction and overall well-being. They broke down breathwork into three distinct categories: cyclic sighing, where you prolong and double your exhale as compared to your inhale or hold; box breathing, where you inhale, hold, and exhale for the same amount of time; and cyclic hyperventilation with retention, where you emphasize a superdeep inhale. The researchers found that breathwork improved mood and helped to calm the breath and heart—but cyclic sighing, with a double exhale, provided the strongest benefit.

Cyclic sighing is an easy method to master—and, again, it takes just a couple of minutes. Sit comfortably, breathe in for four counts, breathe out for four counts, and then exhale twice as if you are trying to empty your lungs. Repeat for several minutes until you feel your heart and breath slow. Not only will it give your mood a boost, but it can also help you move into a more self-aware stance—so you can better examine your life and understand what you need in the moment.

Sometimes when I am feeling brave before a talk at a conference, I'll take two minutes and have the audience do a breathing exercise. As we take some deep breaths with long exhales, I ask everyone to bring their awareness into the room. I've never understood exactly what happens, but each time there is a very powerful shift in the room. We are present with each other and aware . . . and it only takes a few minutes.

ALWAYS HANG IN A SELF-AWARE STANCE

There's no one-size-fits-all approach to self-awareness. And I should also mention that achieving self-awareness is a journey, not a destination. It's something, no matter how well adjusted we may be, that we all need to consistently work on in order to foster Mental Fitness.

I've started the core tenets of Mental Fitness here because self-awareness is so foundational to our efforts in healing the modern brain. We need to be able to see ourselves and our habits objectively in order to understand where we can make changes that will offer us the greatest benefits. And whether you journal, breathe, or just take a step back and try to take a third-person look at a particular situation, you'll find you'll learn important things about yourself and the way you respond to the world around you.

As we move forward, there will be many opportunities to exercise self-awareness. But I would like to mention again that self-awareness should be a judgment-free space. Many of our regular activities, like Charlotte's nightly wine ritual, come about not because we are "bad" or "unhealthy." They develop because we're not paying attention as they transform into automatic habits. When we can be more self-aware, we can pay attention—and understand what it will take to change them. That moves us into a space where we can facilitate both the desire and resources to heal our modern brains.

TIPS FOR INCREASING SELF-AWARENESS

Recognize the Power of Following Up Something Important with the Phrase "I Don't Know." Often, patients who have just shared something very self-aware will follow it with the phrase "I don't know." For example, when Charlotte came to see me, her first words were, "I think I may be drinking too much, I don't know."

Therapists refer to this habit as "disavowal." Meaning, we are emptying out important knowledge we have—and are a little bit uncomfortable as we do so. If you catch yourself doing this, try swapping out the "don't" in "I don't know" for "very clearly" and see how you feel about the preceding statement. When I asked Charlotte to repeat her statement as "I think I may be drinking too much, I very clearly know," it resonated. Her subconscious was trying to tell her something. Maybe yours is trying to tell you something, too.

Take Responsibility. People often complain about institutions or other people. By doing this, we put the blame onto others—we externalize the issue at hand. The problem with this is it's incredibly disempowering. If the problem lies with those other people, we lack the ability to change it. What happens when you take responsibility? When you heighten your awareness around a tendency to externalize problems in your life, you give yourself more control—and the ability to make the changes you need to cultivate better mental health and well-being.

Be Kind to Yourself. Sometimes, self-awareness is hard because it's painful to shine a light on the things that make us feel embarrassed or ashamed. This is where it's important to add in more self-compassion. We all make mistakes. And, when we can learn from them, we can grow into kinder and more empathetic people.

CHAPTER 4

Nutrition

Each day, after Connie, a thirty-eight-year-old marketing professional, returned home from work, she opened the fridge and stared at the stack of premade dinners awaiting her. For the last few months, she'd been receiving ten meals a week from a popular "superfood" meal service. These meals, which are advertised as healthy, nutrient-dense, and appropriately proportioned, heat up in the microwave in under five minutes. When Connie first heard about them—from a fitness influencer she follows on Instagram—she thought they were exactly what she needed to help keep her diet in check.

"I'm so busy at work that I often miss lunch and then would just eat all this junk food when I got home," she said. "These meals are super pricey—but they seemed like they were designed for someone with my lifestyle. Easy, healthy, and fast."

Her description reminded me of my residency days. Overworked and under-rested, I tended to grab whatever takeout was still open on the way home from the hospital—if I hadn't eaten half a cold pizza in the on-call room before leaving. With time at such a premium, healthy eating was at the bottom of my list of priorities. If these kinds of meal services had been available back then, I probably would have signed up myself—if I could have afforded them.

Yet, as Connie continued, it quickly became clear that these meals, as nutrient-dense as they were, were not doing the trick. Every time she goes to reach for one of the meals, even ones that she knows are fairly tasty, Connie said, she just feels deflated. Even the convenience no longer seems worth it.

"I'm paying all this money for these meals so I will actually eat a healthy dinner," Connie said. "But now I'm so bored of them, I end up leaving them in the fridge and ordering in—or just bingeing on whatever junk is in the house. They are just so boring and *joyless*."

As a leading voice in the nutritional psychiatry movement, I've come to understand the power that food can have on brain health. But I hear stories like Connie's far too often. More than ever, people are on the hunt for healthy foods—with a dash of convenience—and find themselves disappointed. That's largely because of all the conflicting and contradictory information we regularly hear about healthy eating. Not to mention the fact that we rarely talk about how to eat for our mental health—and that's interfering with our ability to feed our brains the foods they need to thrive.

Somehow modern nutrition has become, in and of itself, a major barrier to achieving Mental Fitness. This is a sad irony, given the fact that we know more about nutrition and the brain than ever before. Unfortunately, we can't seem to connect the dots to give our brains the nourishment they need. I could point fingers at misleading food marketing, wellness influencers peddling whatever product will pay them, or even well-intentioned meal-delivery start-ups, but much of the blame for this state of affairs falls squarely on us. Historically, we just haven't prioritized feeding the most incredible asset we have—and it's a root cause of our mental suffering.

More and more, when I'm interviewed by members of the media, I'm asked the following question: *Is modern food responsible, at least in part, for our modern mental health epidemic?*

To be honest, I used to get quite twitchy about this question. But with more than a decade of consistent scientific studies showing the role that foods play in brain health, I am more resolute than ever in my answer: Yes. Modern food plays a big role.

Ultraprocessed modern foods, and our relationship with food in general, clearly contribute to the mental health epidemic. Changing the way we eat is one of the most powerful public mental health interventions we can make. It takes some reorientation and adjustment, but overall, approaching brain health in this way is inexpensive, fairly simple, and, most importantly, highly sustainable over the long term.

PROBLEMS WITH THE MODERN DIET

The modern brain is facing a host of new challenges—and many come from our evolving relationship with food.

If you went to school in the United States in the twentieth century, you probably are familiar with the US Department of Agriculture's food pyramid. This representation of basic food groups—grains, fruits and vegetables, dairy, meat and poultry, and fats—first hit school health classes in the early 1990s. It argued that the foundation of a healthy diet, illustrated by the base of the pyramid, involved six to eleven servings of bread, pasta, or other grains *per day*—and suggested that any oils or fats should be eaten sparingly if eaten at all. As you read these words, you can probably conjure the food pyramid, a staple of textbooks and dietary presentations for decades, in your head. It was a fairly easy concept to follow to help you fill your plates.

Today, the USDA has updated the pyramid to an easier-to-follow MyPlate Plan, making it a little more customizable. You can now adjust your plate to account for your age, dietary needs, and budget. But the underlying recommendations are basically the same. And they suffer from the same problem: they don't take into account that all foods aren't created equal. Nutrient density, or the amounts of beneficial vitamins, minerals, complex carbohydrates, lean proteins, and healthy fats contained within a particular food, matters.

It is challenging to heal the modern brain when the way we eat, the way we cook, and the way we nourish our bodies has become so distorted. Over the past one hundred years, our dietary habits have moved from primarily local, farm-fresh foods to prepackaged, processed convenience items. Even Connie's designer meals, which are healthy and fresh as advertised, leave something to be desired. While they are a vast improvement over your mother's go-to Lean Cuisine dinner, they can still leave people feeling uninspired and discouraged.

Somewhere along the way, the food industry changed the way we think about eating. And the overwhelming influence of diet culture doesn't help matters. Far too often, we're told that we shouldn't eat to enjoy, or even eat to live—we should eat to stay slim. That kind of thinking permeates almost every aspect of today's society. Consumers are bombarded with puzzling and often plain inaccurate information about foods and their influence on health and well-being. It's a challenge to sift through all this information to begin with—let alone figure out how to use it to make positive changes in your own diet.

A DE-EVOLUTION IN EATING

Thousands of years ago, long before we settled down and began to rely on central agricultural crops like corn, wheat, and rice, our hunter-gatherer ancestors found food where they could, foraging for edible plants and hunting for game. These people were inextricably linked to the environments they lived in and the foods that naturally existed there. In order to survive, staying put was out of the question. They needed to move with the seasons to stay alive. Thanks to the pioneering work of biological anthropologists, we now know that the average hunter-gatherer diet consisted of about

130 different foods. This is quite a bit of variety—far, far more than our generation of eaters.

About twelve thousand years ago, agricultural practices started to emerge. Hunter-gatherers started to settle down and work the land to grow their food. Yet, even though this meant a big change in the way people ate, the vast majority of each person's sustenance came from local sources and simple, whole ingredients. This was how things were for millennia. Even going back a few generations, our great-grandparents nourished themselves with fresh, seasonal foods that were nurtured on farms within a few dozen miles of their own homes.

Today, however, things have dramatically changed. The American "foodscape" is built on the foundation of industrialized farming operations and ultraprocessed, prepackaged food items. Nearly sixty percent of what the average American consumes falls into the processed-food category—a category rife with excessive levels of refined carbohydrates, food dyes, emulsifiers, and preservatives. You can't drive more than a few blocks without passing a fast-food restaurant or store with shelves full of convenience foods. And our sugar intake—particularly processed sugar—has skyrocketed. In many developed countries, the amount of processed sugar has grown to 150 pounds per person, per year. The types of foods that are most accessible (and often most affordable)—which are actively marketed to you and your family—are chock-full of the very ingredients your doctors strongly warn you to avoid at all costs.

Look at the ingredient labels on many packages in the grocery store and you'll likely see a lot more chemicals—denoted by the long technical names you can't pronounce—than actual food ingredients. Not only does this make it harder for us to eat the nutrients our brains need to help bolster our own mental well-being—the essential nutrients we need that are best received through the consumption of the natural, whole foods that contain them—but the typical Western diet also has us taking in a number of molecules that are detrimental to brain health.

Take fried foods. Many of us have been warned about the danger of fried foods to our physical health, particularly our cardiovascular health, but according to research by the Centers for Disease Control and Prevention (CDC), nearly forty percent of adults in North America consume foods from fast-food restaurants, which are full of fried offerings, every single day. That's a lot of french fries.

But these fried foods do more than just clog our arteries. They can also impact our brain function. One way they do so is through a chemical called acrylamide. Numerous studies have shown that acrylamide, which forms from sugars and amino acids during high-temperature cooking methods like frying, ups your risk of developing cancer as well as cardiovascular disease. The latest studies suggest it plays a role in the development of mental health conditions like anxiety and depression.

Researchers from China's Zhejiang University wanted to understand why the frequent consumption of fried foods—the different variations of fried potatoes in particular—was associated with a higher risk of a depression or anxiety diagnosis. The researchers exposed zebrafish to acrylamide, a by-product created when you fry foods, and then looked at both their behavior and what was happening in their brains.

At first you might think, zebrafish? Really? What can a little bitty fish tell us about human brains? As it turns out, quite a lot. Zebrafish, or *Danio rerio*, are popular models for neuroscientific research. While small in stature, these fish have a nervous system that is similar to that seen in mammals. That's made them a go-to for research labs across the globe that are searching for insights about brain aging, the efficacy of new drugs for brain-related diseases, and, now, how environmental factors can influence brain development and behavior.

After long-term exposure to acrylamide, the fish in the Zhejiang study started acting a little funny. While zebrafish generally like to come out and explore in the sunshine, the animals in the acrylamide group tended to dart out into the light, but then immediately retreat to the darker areas of the fish tank. Zebrafish are also quite social, liking to hang out with their little fishy buddies, forming schools. But not the acrylamide-exposed fish. They tended to hang out all by their lonesome. And zebrafish are also quite curious creatures. Healthy zebrafish will explore their tanks so they can better adapt to the environment. The acrylamide fish, however, stuck to a small area of the tank. Taken together, the researchers believe these behavioral changes suggest something akin to anxiety and depressive symptoms.

When the researchers examined the brains of these fish after the behavioral tests, they found high levels of inflammation. It seems that acrylamide significantly down-regulates the expression of a gene known as *tjp2a*. This gene makes a "tight-junction protein" that acts like molecular glue to hold together the cells of the blood-brain barrier, the protective lining around our brain. Acrylamide exposure also results in changes to how the brain processes important lipids, or fats. All of this contributes to the excess inflammation. And over the past decade, we have come to understand that this inflammation can contribute to depression and anxiety.

In fact, when researchers at Boston's Brigham and Women's Hospital and the Harvard T. H. Chan School of Public Health examined the link between the intake of ultraprocessed-foods, like french fries, and depression, they found that greater consumption was associated with increased risk of depression. Researchers from the Food & Mood Centre at Deakin University in Australia did their own study looking at the relationship between ultraprocessed-food consumption and elevated psychological distress—a measure that is often used to indicate potential depression. Even after controlling for factors like sociodemographic and health characteristics, the group found that those who ate more ultraprocessed foods were more likely to report higher psychological distress, which, over time, would increase the need for a mental health intervention.

As more studies look at how the Western diet affects our brains, one thing is clear: By moving away from whole, nutrient-dense foods, we are doing more than just increasing our risk of cancer and heart disease. We are hurting our brains.

A NOTE ABOUT FOOD MARKETING

I'd be remiss if I didn't mention another factor that has led to our embrace of the Western diet: food marketing. Commercials with fun characters and sticky slogans, especially those we are exposed to as children, stay with us. Don't believe me? Mention Tony the Tiger to any group of people over the age of thirty and I guarantee you that at least one person will bellow, "Theeeeeeeeeeeeeeeeeey're great!" in response. These ads are designed to be memorable for a reason. They want our brains to recognize the bright packaging so we throw the item in our cart while grocery shopping.

Sugary cereals, microwaveable convenience foods, and restaurants collectively spend billions of dollars each year on advertisements—most of which are designed specifically to appeal to children. Take fast-food joints. According to the Rudd Center for Food Policy and Health at the University of Connecticut, fast-food restaurants are increasing their total advertising spend—and buying commercial time during children's television programming. In 2019, they spent $5 billion in total advertising, all but guaranteeing that your kids will see at least two fast-food commercials while they watch television. Kids who spend their time on social media or YouTube are still targeted—with fast-food brands paying for product placements, sponsorships, and interactive engagement opportunities. And while many of these restaurants have promised to offer healthier menu items, their commercials focus on their regular, high-sodium, high-calorie fare.

But that's not our only food marketing foe. While we've known for decades the power that television commercials can have on what foods we decide to buy, we now must also contend with social media influencers. Even Instagram accounts with just a few thousand followers can score sponsorships these days. Sadly, many popular posters in the wellness space are all too happy to talk about "healthy" supplement X or "microbiome-boosting" probiotic powder Y. Not only are your children and teenagers watching these folks, you likely are, too—and they are skewing your understanding of what constitutes healthy eating.

SUPPLEMENT THIS?

At this point, you may be thinking, "Okay, okay—I know I shouldn't be overindulging in certain foods. But I can always make up for it with supplements."

You wouldn't be alone in thinking so. For the last hundred years, many Americans have relied on a daily multivitamin to increase certain levels of vitamins and minerals they may not be getting from the foods they eat. More often than not, their primary care physician is the one who tells them they should start taking it as an "insurance policy."

Certainly, supplements can be helpful in addressing nutrient deficiencies or for individuals with medical conditions that prevent nutrient absorption. They can help you up your vitamin D during the grayer winter months, or up your folate during pregnancy. But it's important to realize that your multivitamin, or any other supplement, cannot fully replace the nutritional value of healthy whole foods.

Today, you can't spend five minutes on social media without seeing ads for pills, powders, and liquids that promise to provide everything your body needs to stay healthy. But the truth of the matter is, even if those products do contain essential vitamins and minerals, your body may not be able to process them. Let me explain. Your body is designed to absorb vital nutrients from food. Common minerals, including nutrients like calcium, magnesium, and iron, can block the uptake of other vitamins and minerals. When you pack two or more of these vitamins into pill, powder, or other form, it often creates a traffic jam in your gut. Your body cannot absorb the full amount contained within the vitamin—so most of that expensive designer supplement will end up just going to waste.

There are other issues with supplements. They aren't well regulated. They are full of adulterants, meaning ingredients that aren't supposed to be in there. The US Food and Drug Administration (FDA) seizes hundreds of different brands of supplements each year for containing toxins, analogues of medications, or even pharmaceutical ingredients. So much for healthy options!

The wrong dosage of certain vitamins can harm you physically, too. Too much vitamin A can lead to liver damage. Megadoses of vitamin D can lead to calcium buildup and kidney stones. And when you ingest too much magnesium, it can cause gastrointestinal issues. By trying to get your nutrients in pill form, you may end up causing more harm than benefit. I'd also add that it's hard to know if vitamins help. So often, when patients come to see me and I ask about what medications or supplements they are taking, they start listing half a dozen or more items. With so many different supplements, there's no way to really know what is helping and what isn't. Worse, because the label says "healthy" or "natural," people think these supplements are good for the brain when, in reality, it's usually not the case.

I'm not saying that you should toss the supplement your doctor suggested you take. But what I am saying is that, as you consider how to obtain the nutrients your body and brain need, your first thought should be about what whole foods can provide them. Because what's happening is, instead of securing vital nutrients found naturally in whole foods that provide the building blocks of healthy brains, we are instead ingesting a host of manufactured foodlike substances. And they aren't doing the trick. According to the US Department of Agriculture (USDA), the vast majority of Americans are not meeting the recommended daily allowance (RDA) for key nutrients. Studies show that about fifty percent of us fall short on zinc. Sixty-eight percent are deficient in magnesium intake. And seventy-five percent are not managing to eat enough of the crucial folate their brains need to work their best. And let's not forget about vitamin E. This fat-soluble vitamin is a power player in terms of protecting our brains. Yet ninety-six percent of American eaters don't even come close to meeting the recommended daily allowance of this essential vitamin! We need these basic elements to flourish. And the best way to obtain them is through whole, nutrient-dense foods.

The key is knowing which foods you can find them in.

It's not always easy. That's one of the reasons I wrote *Eat Complete: The 21 Nutrients That Fuel Brainpower, Boost Weight Loss, and Transform Your Health* and *Eat to Beat Depression and Anxiety: Nourish Your Way to Better Mental Health in Six Weeks*. Both books not only provide a clear illustration of the concepts behind nutritional psychiatry, helping you to better understand the food categories that bolster brain health, but also offer clear guidance and recipes to easily add brain-boosting vitamins and minerals to your daily meals.

THE OTHER FOOD ELEPHANTS IN THE ROOM

It would be nice if we only had to contend with processed foods and supplements. But eating in the modern world also comes with other major pitfalls that can affect our brain function. Diet culture is toxic. We are trained, from an early age, to eat to be skinny instead of healthy. Our doctors often tell us that we should be eating to be smaller, too. Felice Jacka, a researcher at Australia's Food & Mood Centre, and a true pioneer in the study of how nutrition influences mental health, said this is one of her biggest pet peeves.

"So much of the messaging around food has been around the obesity epidemic and people's body size," she said. "We need to get away from this idea that nutrition is about body size and appearance—which is very stigmatizing. Instead, we should be telling people to nourish their brains, their guts, their bodies, and their spirits. This is something wonderful you can do for yourself— eating shouldn't be about punishment, restriction, or misery."

Every year, there's a new, trendy diet that hits the mainstream. More often than not, this year's hot take on what we should eat contradicts what last year's healthy diet said we should do. These fad diets do incredible damage to our self-esteem and well-being by consistently telling us that we're eating all wrong. They take their toll on our brains, too.

In addition to the skinny-to-be-healthy mindset, there are also literal toxins in our foods. Food-processing practices can result in all manner of toxins being inadvertently added to the foods we eat regularly. While such concerns were once deemed hysterical, the latest scientific studies show the effects are irrefutable. Exposure to persistent organic pollutants like polychlorinated biphenyl (PCB), dioxin, and bisphenol A comes from foods.

Simultaneously, microplastics are multiplying in our marine supply chains—and our favorite herbal tea bags. Researchers found that the latest tea bags, which look quite fancy and keep tea fresh, spew one to two billion microplastic particles into your brew.

The end result of all this—the mix of our skewed cultural values and the potent misconceptions about what constitutes healthy food—is that eating is inextricably linked to shame and fear. And for the millions of people who already struggle with anxiety, the conflicting and often scary information about what to eat (and what not to eat) may make them even more fretful about their food choices. Is it any wonder that Connie decided to just invest in a meal service, joyless as it may be? When it feels like your food choices are something that you'll never get right, you end up going for what's easiest.

We need to find a way to go back to consuming whole foods, complete with the healthy nutrients our brains need, to heal the modern brain.

BUILDING BLOCKS FOR BRAIN HEALTH

You've likely heard the old adage "You are what you eat." As it so happens, when it comes to your brain, that old chestnut is largely true. Our brains are made of the very same things that natural foods are made of. Neurotransmitters and receptors are constructed of specific proteins and amino acids. Minerals like zinc, selenium, and magnesium provide the building blocks for your brain cells and surrounding tissues. They also provide essential ingredients to create neurotransmitters and other important neuromodulatory molecules. Sodium and potassium are minerals that help our brains conduct nerve impulses—and send important communications between cells to support thought, emotion, and behavior.

Your body does not make any of these minerals on its own. You need to obtain them from the foods you eat. When your diet is missing these items, cognition, mood, and overall brain function will suffer. Consider serotonin. You already know that serotonin is a mood enhancer. If your diet doesn't provide foods with adequate levels of nutrients like iron, folate, and vitamin B_{12}, you won't make enough of it. You increase your risk of developing depression.

For far too long, physicians did not include food in health assessments—and forget about trying to determine whether people were eating to promote mental health. Until recently, we simply didn't know what nutrients were most important to feed our brains.

To understand which nutrients are most important in mental health, particularly depression, my colleague Laura R. LaChance, MD, and I conducted a systematic review to determine the most important vitamins and minerals—as well as the foods that contain them in the highest densities. Nutrient density, simply defined, is the amount of nutrients you ingest per calorie in a food. Understanding a food's nutrient density is now a foundational principle for me. As far as I'm concerned, the only reason to ever count calories of food is to be able to calculate how nutrient-dense it is.

Understanding nutrient density is important. Your food choices determine what sort of building materials your brain has on hand. And to help heal the modern brain, it pays to make choices that contain the following vital nutrients. I got deeper into the mental health effects and top food sources along with nutrient-dense recipes in my previous books. Here are some highlights.

Folate

It's not just for expectant mothers anymore! There's a reason why pregnancy vitamins include a healthy dose of folate, a type of B vitamin. It helps support the creation and development of new cells and is vital for making important neurotransmitters like serotonin. You can find it in foods like brussels sprouts, oranges, and leafy greens. But one of my favorite sources of folate is lentils.

Iron

Your brain runs on oxygenated blood. That means iron is your brain's best friend. Iron is an important component of hemoglobin, the protein in red blood cells that helps transport oxygen from the lungs to the brain. You also need iron to make the neurotransmitter dopamine. Iron is easily accessible in any type of meat. But you can also find ample stores of this mineral in foods like pumpkin seeds, cashews, oysters, and Popeye's go-to meal, spinach.

Long-Chained Omega-3 Fatty Acids

It's a long name, no doubt. But these long-chain polyunsaturated fatty acids (try saying that ten times fast), including eicosapentaenoic acid (EPA) and docosahexaenoic acid (DHA), help provide the brain with the building and insulating materials that facilitate neural transmission. Your body makes some of these fatty acids naturally in the liver—but not enough to help the brain work its best. You should increase your stores by consuming seafood, including wild salmon, anchovies, oysters, and algae.

Magnesium
This mineral is purported to help calm the nervous system. People often talk about magnesium as a sleep aid. But this mineral also helps regulate important neurotransmitters, including serotonin and others that help support mood. You can find magnesium in beans, spinach, almonds, and cashews.

Potassium
If the mere mention of the Na+/K+ pump gives you high school biology flashbacks, I apologize. But K+, or potassium, is required for every electrical impulse that travels along a neuron. Bananas are a great source of this mineral. But you can find it in other fresh fruits and vegetables, including broccoli, sweet potatoes, and white beans.

Selenium
When you think about healthy vitamins and minerals, selenium may not be the first name that comes to mind. But this trace mineral helps to create a powerful antioxidant to support brain health. It also plays an significant role in the proper functioning of the thyroid gland, an important part of your body's endocrine system. The hormones released by the thyroid help to regulate mood and energy levels—and also help fight against anxiety. You can find selenium in foods like oatmeal, oysters, Brazil nuts, and mushrooms.

Thiamine (B$_1$)
The first vitamin to be identified, thiamine is fundamental to brain health. It helps to convert the carbohydrates you eat into a form of

energy that the body—and the brain—can use. If you are a carnivore, beef is a great source of thiamine. But you can also find it in nuts and legumes.

Vitamin A

A healthy brain is a plastic brain—one that can grow, adapt, and change in response to the environment to help you learn and thrive. Several studies have now linked vitamin A to neuroplasticity. If you are looking for foods that contain this vitamin, check out brightly colored fruits and vegetables, including corn, bell peppers, tomatoes, watermelon, cantaloupe, carrots, and broccoli. You'll also find vitamin A in seafoods like mackerel and wild-caught salmon. (I'd be remiss if I didn't add that liver is also a fantastic source of this vitamin.)

Vitamin B$_6$

Another of the B vitamins, B$_6$ plays a pivotal role in brain development as a cofactor. Cofactors are vitamins and minerals that help catalyze the chemical reactions that help our cells to make important molecules like neurotransmitters. You can find B$_6$ in eggs, pistachios, and several whole grains.

Vitamin B$_{12}$

Add B$_{12}$ to the list of brain-boosting nutrients. This B vitamin— the largest of the vitamins that our bodies can absorb—is central to the production of mood-regulating neurotransmitters like serotonin, norepinephrine, and dopamine. It also helps to support the myelination of brain cells—the insulation that helps cells transmit signals more efficiently and effectively. Clams, liver, and mussels are all high in B$_{12}$.

Vitamin C

You already know that vitamin C is an immune booster. This powerful antioxidant can also counteract the damage caused by free radicals in brain cells. You also already know you can find plenty of vitamin C in oranges. But cherries, chilies, red peppers, and mustard greens also contain a good dose of this vitamin.

Zinc

This is the unsung hero of brain nutrients. This mineral helps to regulate brain signaling and neuroplasticity. Most of us aren't eating enough zinc. Luckily, you can increase your zinc levels by adding pumpkin seeds, oysters, and turkey to your diet.

EMBRACING ESSENTIAL FOOD CATEGORIES

You can boost your Mental Fitness with the addition of these twelve nutrients. But understanding that these vitamins and minerals are important to boosting your brain health may not do much in the way of changing your diet. Telling people that they need to eat more iron, zinc, or B$_{12}$ can only take you so far. Bolstering your Mental Fitness requires more than just adding the latest superfood to your plate. To help the brain work its best, it's more valuable to think more broadly about food categories.

Eating to heal the modern brain isn't about powders, supplements, or adding the superfood du jour to your diet. While blueberries, green tea, spirulina, and matcha are all great foods, packed with the healthy nutrients that promote brain health, they aren't the end-all-be-all when it comes to Mental Fitness. You need a wide range of different foods to hit all the necessary nutrients. I'd also add that you should pick the foods you enjoy eating. No one should have to open their fridge each night like Connie and detest their options for dinner. From my point of view, the only must-have component of a brain-healthy diet, besides unprocessed foods, is a certain amount of joy. After all, food is meant to be delicious. It's meant to add some pleasure to your daily lives. I'm here to tell you that you can eat to boost your brain—and actually enjoy it. You *should* enjoy it.

You've likely heard a lot about the Mediterranean diet. Many doctors, including myself, prescribe it for patients—and for good reason. This style of eating is inspired by the traditional foods and eating habits of the Mediterranean region. It's low in processed foods and high in fresh fruits and vegetables—not to mention nuts, legumes, seafoods, and olive oil. Study after study has shown that it's not only good for your heart, but good for your brain. And it lowers your risk for depression, anxiety, and overall psychological distress.

Clinical trials show the power of the Mediterranean diet to reverse mental health symptoms, too. For example, Jacka demonstrated that providing people diagnosed with depression dietary counseling and support, helping study participants to start eating a modified version of the Mediterranean diet, could reduce symptoms over the course of twelve weeks. Another group of Aussie researchers provided the Mediterranean diet as an intervention in male patients who had been diagnosed with moderate to severe depression. After twelve weeks, the participants saw significant improvements in their symptoms. The Mediterranean diet is a great way to obtain those twelve essential nutrients, with their real, observable effects on the brain, out of the scientific literature and onto your plate. It's also a highly enjoyable way of eating. But, with that in mind, you don't have to follow the Mediterranean diet—or any other diet, for that matter—to the letter. You can focus on the following important food categories to help ensure your brain is getting the vitamins and minerals necessary to thrive.

Leafy Greens

You probably knew this one was coming. But when it comes to getting the most bang for your buck, nutrient-wise, leafy greens have an incredible nutrient-to-calorie ratio. The foundation of your plate should be made up of spinach, kale, watercress, arugula, collards, beet greens, and chard. That's what will give you your daily dose of vitamins C and A, as well as plenty of folate.

Rainbow Fruits and Vegetables

Nutritionists often recommend that you "eat the rainbow." And for good reason! By eating colorful fruits and veggies, like tomatoes, bell peppers, avocados, broccoli, and berries, you can consume important phytonutrients that help support brain health—but you should also eat ample fiber to feed the good bugs in your microbiome.

Seafood

I know that not everyone likes seafood. But it's the only food category where you can ingest the long-chain omega-3 fatty acids that your brain so desperately needs. Sardines, oysters, mussels, and salmon are also chock-full of B_{12}, selenium, iron, zinc, and protein. While fish may not be your favorite food, there are a variety of ways to enjoy and experience seafood. With some trial and error, you can, no doubt, find the one that fits your brain just right.

Nuts, Seeds, and Legumes

Cashews, lentils, and pumpkin seeds, oh my! These incredible sources of plant-based protein offer fiber, zinc, iron, and other essential nutrients. One of the first things I suggest to patients is replacing their current go-to snack with some almonds, walnuts, and cashews. Even a handful of these power-packed foods can go a long way to improving your brain health.

Meat

This is another tricky category, especially since many people prefer a plant-based diet. That said, meat is a remarkable source of iron, protein, and vitamin B_{12}. As such, I've come to believe that the age-old debate over whether we should or shouldn't eat meat should evolve into a conversation about how to eat meat in a way that is healthy and sustainable for both our bodies and the planet. When you add grass-fed beef to your diet, you aren't just getting protein. You are also eating foods that contain the healthier fats, vitamin E, and carotenoids that the animals eat as they roam and eat natural vegetation.

Egg

They don't call the egg incredible for nothing! At a mere seventy calories, this incredibly affordable and simple food is an almost ideal protein. It also contains B vitamins and choline, both of which are linked to decreased mood and anxiety symptoms.

Fermented Foods

The latest research into gut-brain connections shows us that having a diverse microbiome—or a diverse population of healthy bacteria in your gastrointestinal track—helps to keep the brain healthy. By consuming fermented foods like kombucha, kefir, yogurt, sauerkraut, kimchi, miso, and natto, you can consume live probiotic bacteria to help ensure your gut is full of "good bugs" that can help bolster your mood and your overall Mental Fitness.

Dark Chocolate

I've saved the best for last! Dark chocolate is not only delicious, but a remarkable source of flavanols like epicatechin, a molecule that has both cardiovascular and brain health benefits. People who eat higher amounts of dark chocolate have a seventy percent reduction in risk for clinically relevant depression symptoms. Look for a product with cacao content of at least seventy percent. The higher the percentage of cacao, the better it is for your brain.

These are the food categories that will help put your brain in grow mode, facilitating the production and release of brain-fertilizing molecules like brain-derived neurotrophic factor (BDNF). They are the foods that are high in the nutrients that can help reduce inflammation and thus help reduce mental health symptoms. They are also the foods that feed your microbiome, ensuring you maintain a healthy and diverse population of good bugs. Put them all together and you have a recipe for improved mood and mental health.

But just as Rome wasn't built in a day, no one is expecting you to completely overhaul your diet after reading this chapter. Instead, you can start simple—and make a few substitutes or swaps to increase the nutrients your brain needs to thrive.

NOURISHING YOUR BRAIN

When Connie first came to see me, she was battling anxiety. By the time she returned home from work each day, she was exhausted from the effort involved in "acting normal." Anxiety also interfered with her appetite, leading her to excessively worry about how many grams of protein she was consuming. This combination of symptoms made her especially vulnerable to Instagram influencers. That's why she opted for this easy meal service. It's also why she was a big fan of protein powders and nutrition bars. She wanted to make it as easy as possible to eat the nutrients she needed to feel her best.

But here's the problem: many of the foods that are marketed to us all as "healthy," "natural," "multigrain," or "gluten-free" are still ultraprocessed. And while they may be convenient—and make you feel like you are doing the right thing when you hit the grocery store each week—these foods may be hurting us as much as grabbing our favorite traditional junk fare.

Case in point: When Jacka and her colleagues dove deeper into the data from the SMILES trial, they found something interesting. They decided to look at each participant's food diary and estimate the proportion of ultraprocessed foods, in grams, in their overall diet. They found that for each ten percent reduction in ultraprocessed foods, they saw a significant improvement in the metric they used to measure depressive symptoms. The fewer ultraprocessed foods the participants ate, the better their mood. It's a striking finding.

"So often people don't recognize that they are eating an ultraprocessed food when they are consuming out of a box—they think it's a pasta meal or a pizza and it's okay," said Jacka. "But these foods are created by taking the original food apart, breaking it down into all these different constituents, and then reformulating it. It has extra ingredients like emulsifiers, preservatives, and lots of different additives. And that's hugely problematic. Our work has shown that when people are eating a lot of ultraprocessed food, they consume, on average, five hundred extra calories a day. These foods seem to somehow bypass the body's natural appetite regulation systems—and they also interact with the brain's reward systems to prompt people to eat more of them. While this is great for the pockets of the large multinational corporations that make these foods, it's really, really terrible for our health."

And so, to help Connie—as well as most of my other patients—I recommend skipping the foods that come in boxes or plastic wrappers. There are plenty of other ways to add nutrient-dense foods to your diet without relying on the food-industrial complex, without having to think too hard about what you are making.

Let's start with breakfast. Connie would usually grab some coffee and a "keto-friendly" nutrition bar. Instead, I suggested she start out her day with a smoothie. By putting together the ingredients she needs in the fridge the night before—and using frozen fruit to make things convenient—she can simply dump, blend, and go.

While there are a lot of smoothie recipes out there, most are nothing more than glorified sugar bombs. But a classic brain-boosting smoothie is simply a base of kefir, a fermented dairy product, with some blueberries, basil, and some pumpkin seeds. All of these foods are high in the nutrients that your brain needs the most. You have the kefir to keep the "good bugs" in your microbiome happy. The blueberries and basil have a lot of healthy phytonutrients. And the pumpkin seeds are not only high in tryptophan, zinc, and magnesium—they also add a nice dash of extra creaminess to this morning meal.

This is a basic recipe. But you can mix it up based on what fruits are in season—and what you are in the mood for. Pick your favorite fruits. Throw in some kale or spinach to eat your leafy greens. Instead of pumpkin seeds, try some walnuts or chia seeds. You can mix and match. But whatever you choose, you'll have the fiber, fats, and greens to feed your microbiome and brain. And if you aren't a smoothie person? You can make similar mixes using overnight oats.

Now let's think about lunch. Most of the time, people hear about the importance of increasing leafy-green consumption and automatically assume that means eating more salads. Now, I do recommend what I call a brain-bow salad. You throw in your favorite green—kale, arugula, Swiss chard, or spinach. Then add in some small red beans, avocado, egg, and colorful veggies. By adding these different essential food categories, you are giving your brain all the nutrients it needs to stay fighting fit. You are also eating the protein and fats to remain full and satisfied.

That said, I understand not everyone is a salad person. You can eat leafy greens—as well as foods from the other essential categories—in the ways that you enjoy them the most. You can sauté greens with some olive oil and garlic and top with some salmon or steak. You can add all manner of colorful veggies, including leafy greens, into your favorite soups or stews. But my favorite way to eat my greens is by blending them into a nice pesto. You can easily add it to some fresh seafood, chicken, or even some fresh pasta topped off with fresh rainbow veggies.

Finally, I like to also make sure my dessert includes a dash of brain food. I heartily recommend dark chocolate. This is not a guilty treat, meant to be eaten where no one can see you. It's a food that we know feeds our brains. I eat it almost every day. One of my favorite ways to indulge is by making brain truffles. I put together dates, nuts, dark chocolate, and cacao nibs, and roll them into a ball. These are the kind of sweet treats that give you the magnesium, fiber, zinc, and B vitamins your body needs. You can get your nutrition in each and every delicious, dark chocolaty bite.

BUT WHAT ABOUT KETOSIS?

You may have noticed that we haven't talked about ketogenic diets in this chapter. These days, it seems like every celebrity is talking about the power of keto, or a high-fat, medium-protein, low-carbohydrate diet to shed pounds and increase energy. The idea is that it puts your body into a state of ketosis, which, in theory, instructs the body to burn fat at a high rate. But the omission of keto recommendations is intentional. While there are some studies that show that ketogenic diets can help patients with epilepsy or bipolar disorder to better control their symptoms, there's very little scientific evidence to show any further brain benefits. A 2024 pilot study of twenty-three patients with schizophrenia or bipolar disorder showed significant improvements in mental and physical health when the participants followed a ketogenic diet. But the study was quite small—so all we can say with any real certainty is that further study is needed to see if it may be of benefit to mental health. The jury is still out—and until there are larger controlled trials to show it is effective, Jacka said it's best to stick with what we know works well for the brain.

"There seems to be a widespread misunderstanding that carbohydrates are bad—people are somehow conflating donuts with sweet potatoes or oats," said Jacka. "And the fact is that the ketogenic diet can be quite dangerous for some people. You need a lot of guidance from a dietitian to do it in a way that won't cause nutritional problems. That's not to say that there's not potential for this kind of diet to be helpful, but we need to generate the evidence base first."

Jacka added that another issue with the ketogenic diet today is that many followers turn to ultraprocessed foods to meet the incredibly restrictive rules.

"When you look at the ketogenic diet, it really is the

opposite of what the evidence tells us about eating for mental health and gut health," she said. "Unless you are following a very careful diet that is explicitly designed to address fiber, polyphenols, and healthy fats, you are missing out on the nutrients that your brain needs to work its best."

EATING FOR MENTAL FITNESS

I've spent a lot of time in this chapter talking about nutrients and the best food categories in which to find them—and for good reason. But eating to heal the modern brain is more than just your food choices. It means never having to open your fridge to another joyless, boring dinner. It involves eating the foods you like to eat. It's about being more social and enjoying your meals with friends and family. It's finding ways to add whole foods to your diet—and maybe even empowering yourself to learn how to prepare the foods you love in the ways you love them.

I'd also add that eating for Mental Fitness does not have to be expensive—despite what your favorite social media influencer may be trying to sell you. Going back to the SMILES trial, Felice Jacka and her colleagues decided to look at more than just what kinds of foods people were eating—they also did a full economic evaluation of making the suggested dietary improvements. They discovered that the study participants saved, on average, about twenty-five dollars per week on food—but a deeper dive into the data also showed other remarkable savings.

"We had a health economist who looked at all sorts of data and showed that there was roughly a two-and-a-half-thousand Australian-dollar cost saving per participant," Jacka explained. "This was more than just what people were spending on food. They also noted that people in the dietary group spent a lot less time outside their daily roles and saw health practitioners less often. So, the change in diet was not just helping their mental health; it had a much more global impact on their health."

I know that food is complicated—and there are far too many myths and misconceptions floating around about what healthy eating is. But you can eat for brain health both economically and joyously. And you can do it in a way that works for you.

In my clinical work, I've learned that different people need different things to eat to boost brain health. Some people need a friend or family member to help them come up with the right recipes and support them as they work to add more nutrient-dense foods to the mix. Others need the structure of a cooking class. (That's one reason why I started a digital cooking class, the Mental Fitness Kitchen.) Still others might benefit from working with a registered dietitian to help find the right substitutions and add-ons.

That said, as you look to heal the modern brain, I'm here to tell you that you won't find what you are looking for in the supplement bottle or in a glorified TV dinner. They may be convenient, but they aren't really what your brain needs. You can nourish your body—and your brain—by making some simple swaps and finding ways to enhance the foods you already enjoy with some nutrient-dense options. (For readers who would like more detailed guidance, including recipes and meal plans, let me point you to *Eat Complete: The 21 Nutrients That Fuel Brainpower, Boost Weight Loss, and Transform Your Health* and *Eat to Beat Depression and Anxiety: Nourish Your Way to Better Mental Health in Six Weeks*.)

You can find joy in eating again. And, in the process, support your Mental Fitness both nutritiously and deliciously.

CHAPTER 5

Movement

My uncle Bob has always been an early adopter.

A psychiatrist himself, he was the first adult I knew to not only appreciate the importance of physical fitness to support a healthier lifestyle, but to integrate regular exercise into his busy life. Back in the early 1990s, he turned his basement man cave, complete with big-screen television and surround sound system, into an at-home gym. Behind the couch where my cousins and I would spend hours playing video games he placed a stationary bike, a rowing machine, and—the pièce de résistance—a NordicTrack, an awkward cardio contraption that was meant to mimic cross-country skiing. Each Sunday, if the weather was too poor for outdoor activities, Uncle Bob would invite his two best friends to come over to work out. As an action movie blared in the background (usually *Die Hard*, or something else starring the macho and versatile Bruce Willis), he and his buddies would get their sweat on, taking turns on the different machines for twenty-minute intervals until the movie was over.

This was my introduction to "fitness" training. While others might have been inspired by Jane Fonda or the local Jazzercise class, I had a brownstone basement and a bunch of middle-aged guys trying to reclaim their athletic glory days.

The summer I turned fifteen, after proving myself as a reason-ably sturdy student athlete on the pole vault, my uncle invited me to join the Sunday exercise enclave. I was *pumped*. Each time I vis-ited for the weekend, I would stand on the side of the couch, doing some bicep curls with a couple of free weights, until it was my turn to hop on one of the pieces of cardio equipment. But, as excited as I was to participate in what I then perceived as quite manly feats of strength, I realized I really didn't like working out on the ma-chines. The NordicTrack felt alien to me. Even after finding some kind of rhythm perched on the "skis," I never felt quite right. I kept staring at my feet, wondering if I looked as ridiculous as I felt trying to keep my balance on the rickety machine. I didn't fare much better on the rowing machine. I could never quite get into a groove, alternating between pulling the bar too hard or somehow coming up short. But even pedaling on the stationary bike, which my body instinctively knew how to do thanks to all the miles I cov-ered on my Schwinn back home, felt like a chore. I'd look down at the timer, impatiently waiting for my time interval to finish. Not even the loud and fast-paced car chases on the big screen could distract me from my bored torment. Trying to raise my heart rate on the road to nowhere, regardless of whatever equipment I used, just felt clumsy and annoying.

As I tried to pedal my hardest on the stationary bike, I couldn't help but think of how Uncle Bob and I spent our time on Chicago's mild and sunny days. On those Sundays, Uncle Bob would can-cel the basement fitness party and tell my cousins and me to grab our bikes. We'd take off for the paths surrounding Lake Michigan, ready and willing to take full advantage of the good weather. We'd ride for miles, enjoying the sunshine and camaraderie. On one of those epic Sunday rides, I realized we'd been gone for almost three hours. We'd all been having so much fun, racing along the paths and just taking in the scenery, that I hadn't realized how much time had passed. Honestly, I would have eagerly continued riding for a while longer.

I wondered, even then, why I could only, at best, tolerate my rides on the stationary bike. I would spend my time counting down the seconds until my interval was up. On outdoor rides, however, I could seemingly go on forever. I'd lose myself in the full experience of the tour. While I might acutely feel the effort of having to pump the pedals harder to go uphill or catch one of my cousins as we raced, the discomfort never lingered. Riding outside, even when you figured in the extra time or mileage, just felt different. It was natural and fun. I'd go so far as to call it joyful, even.

Moving my body in this manner did more than just keep my heart rate up for the recommended moderate-intensity exercise period suggested by health experts to keep my body and brain healthy. It made me feel good. It helped me get out of my head. It allowed me to decompress—and focus on something other than whatever intrusive thoughts were making it so I was getting in my own way. I found these outdoor bike rides so beneficial that once I moved to New York City, I'd commute to work each day on my bike. It was a mere ten-minute journey, not a "workout" by any stretch of the imagination. But I'd find myself put at ease as I rode, pedaling as fast as I could to outmaneuver the city traffic and catch each light as I made my way to and from the clinic. Even better were the nights when I didn't have to rush home. That's when I'd extend my ride by several miles, heading downtown and then circling back up the island again, giving myself the time and space to move, release, and just *be*.

THE EXERCISE PARADOX (OR EXERCISE IN THE MODERN WORLD)

We all know that exercise is good for us. Log into social media, open your favorite news site, or browse what's left of the magazine rack at the supermarket checkout and you'll see no end to articles about the best ways to embrace fitness, shed pounds, and optimize your health.

There are also plenty of options available to help you achieve your recommended daily allotment of exercise each week. You can spin, lift, or row. You can train for a marathon or triathlon. You can rock your core with Pilates or chase your Zen with yoga or a little tai chi. And don't forget the wide variety of options—as well as hybrid offerings—that support climbing, skiing, boxing, swimming, dancing, kayaking, walking, jogging, riding, jumping, skating, and hiking activities. The possibilities for exercise these days are seemingly endless.

Decades after the aerobics revolution of the 1980s—which is about the time Uncle Bob designed his basement gym—the fitness industry ballooned into a gluttonous behemoth, with profits in excess of $100 billion annually. Across the globe, people are spending a good chunk of their disposable income on machines, weights, memberships, trainers, supplements, and classes. Yet, with all this money—not to mention individual and collective time and effort—spent on exercise, we are way less active and physically fit than our parents and grandparents were. Let me repeat that: we are way less active and physically fit than our parents and grandparents were. Despite the myriad of exercise options available to us, we aren't seeing the benefits we hope to see.

We have also adopted a strange tone when we talk about exercise. We go out of our way to tell ourselves that exercise is supposed to hurt. Your local gym or exercise hot spot likely has a T-shirt festooned with slogans like NO PAIN, NO GAIN or PAIN IS JUST WEAKNESS LEAVING THE BODY. Instagram and other social media platforms are full of pain platitudes. The fitness influencers, in between trying to sell you some kind of product, make sure to repeatedly tell you that the pain you feel today is the strength you'll feel tomorrow. To use your pain as fuel to keep going. What started as weight-room talk has now become part and parcel of almost every exercise regimen. To be healthier, you are not only supposed to accept pain, but welcome it. Do more. Do it harder. Make it hurt. Let's face it: if we used this kind of talk to describe any other kind of relationship, we'd likely consider it a rather loud cry for help.

The official recommendations for cardiovascular exercise are somewhat straightforward. The Centers for Disease Control and Prevention recommend 150 minutes of aerobic activity per week, dryly stating: "It has been estimated that people who are physically active for approximately 150 minutes a week have a thirty-three percent lower risk of all-cause mortality than those who are not physically active." Other guidelines state that adults should "move more and sit less" throughout the day. But none of the official takes on exercise discuss *what* we should do or at what *intensity* we should do it. That means that far too many people feel like the activities they enjoy don't meet the criteria. The end result? We end up doing more exercises we don't really like, for a longer time—and then still feel guilty about it.

This is physical fitness in the modern world. Is it any wonder that so many of us feel underlying dread when it comes time to work out? We're smack-dab in the middle of an exercise paradox. We are supposed to hurt ourselves to heal ourselves. And even then, we somehow aren't doing *enough*.

Somewhere along the way, our views on movement, our relationships with exercise, and our everyday habits became profoundly skewed. It's taking a toll on our brains—and, consequently, our ability to achieve Mental Fitness.

EVOLVED TO MOVE

It's probably no surprise that our ancestors moved more than we do. They had to: it was a matter of survival. The need to gather food, escape predators, and thrive in a variety of different environments shaped the way both our bodies and brains evolved. Facilitating the ability to get enough to eat, protect ourselves and our families, and, of course, propagate the species fundamentally shaped our human physiology.

On average, your average hunter-gatherer would cover roughly seven miles per day. That's what it took to scrape out a meager subsistence. If people didn't move, they didn't eat. Contrast that with today's mileage. The average American has difficulty managing four thousand steps (the equivalent of about two miles) from sunup to sundown. Our great-grandparents and grandparents didn't clock their daily steps the way we do but they, too, were far more active than our generation. Occupations in farming, skilled labor, and industry demanded it.

Today we are far more sedentary. According to the National Institutes of Health, nearly eighty percent of modern jobs in the United States involve "mostly sedentary activities"—and it is giving rise to "colossal" inactivity. You may already be thinking: *I've already read a couple of articles about this. My doctor keeps mentioning exercise at my annual physical. My mailbox is full of gym membership offers. I understand. Exercise is good. Can we please move on?*

You are correct that there is no lack of public outreach and discourse surrounding the need for increased physical activity and exercise. But the vast majority of that focuses solely on exercise's relation to overall body health—how it affects the heart, the lungs, and muscular composition. There are all manner of studies showing that a regular exercise regimen is linked to a reduced risk of disease ranging from type 2 diabetes to cancer. Despite those studies, however, most of the chatter comes down to exercise's influence on body-fat percentage. There's a subliminal message in there that it doesn't necessarily matter if you're healthy provided you are slim. That's a shame.

Beyond the whole health/thinness dichotomy, however, we also miss another crucial element when we discuss the importance of exercise. We've spent so much time discussing what exercise can do for your heart and waistline, we've neglected the organ that may benefit the most: your brain.

That's right. Your brain is made for movement. The human

brain has a huge amount of real estate dedicated to motor function and control. And for good reason: it helped our hunter-gatherer ancestors not just survive but thrive in the face of an ever-changing environment. Our brains learn from movement. Our brains respond to movement. Our brains crave it. And that's why introducing even small amounts of exercise into our daily lives can have crucial, monumental effects on our mental well-being.

MOVING YOUR BRAIN INTO GROW MODE

Let's take a quick look at what happens in the brain as you engage in moderate aerobic exercise. This could be a thirty-minute bike ride, a game of pickup basketball, or a walk in the woods. The very act of moving changes your physiology in a variety of ways.

Increased Blood Flow

As you increase your effort, your heart rate goes up, too. There's a purpose to this elevated heart rate. It helps to move blood, and thus oxygen, to your muscles so they can keep going. While the brain is not a muscle (though it is often referred to as such), that extra oxygenated blood is also of benefit.

It's important to understand that the brain is a bit of an energy hog. As our cardiovascular system works to move blood around the body, the brain will take about twenty to twenty-five percent of the oxygen and fuel that blood carries. Given that the average brain is only about three pounds—an estimated two percent of the body's size—this looks, at first, to be a rather unfair arrangement. But our brains need as much of that oxygen as possible so neurons can work at their best. That's the first way that movement helps our brains.

Neurogenesis

Rusty Gage, PhD, has been studying brain plasticity since he started his career in neuroscience more than four decades ago. As a professor at the Salk Institute, he's interested in ways to prevent neurodegeneration—and he uses animal models to see if different activities can help keep the brain hale and hearty even as mammals age.

At the turn of the twenty-first century, Gage found that mice who lived in enriched environments—think space to roam, toys to play with, tubes to hide in, and wheels to run on—not only were better at learning than animals who were housed in unequipped old cages, their brains were fundamentally different, too. An area of the brain called the dentate gyrus, which is adjacent to the brain's memory center, the hippocampus, was fifteen percent bigger. The dentate gyrus plays a vital role in learning, transferring information to the hippocampus so it can be stored in memory. Seeing this significant increase in volume in adult mice piqued Gage's curiosity. What aspect of enrichment might be responsible for this kind of neuronal growth? He and his colleagues aimed to find out by separating the different activities. After a series of meticulous studies, Gage and his team found that animals that had free access to running wheels saw the biggest brain growth. The activity increased the proliferation of neurons in the dentate gyrus. They also noted that these animals were better at learning simple tasks—and had enhanced long-term potentiation, or the persistent strengthening of synapses that supports memory.

Gage's work was just the beginning. And in the quarter century since, neuroscientists across the globe have studied how movement affects the brain. They've learned that physical activity facilitates the growth of new neurons and allows the brain to form and strengthen neural circuits. And while Gage's studies initially suggested that running was the act that was putting the brain in grow mode, the truth is, subsequent studies have shown even just a little movement goes a long way in helping to increase cell growth and brain volume.

Endorphins, Neurotransmitters, and Growth Factors

Also contributing to brain-growth mode are important neuromodulators, or molecules that help to change the way that our neurons grow and communicate with one another. Exercise facilitates the release of endorphins. These are special hormones that can activate the body's opiate receptors. While they don't exactly offer the same punch as heroin, the release of movement-related endorphins has been linked to elevated mood and decreased perception of pain.

Exercise is also linked to the release of powerful neurotransmitters, or electrochemical messengers that carry messages between your brain cells. Those communications are the foundation of every thought, every feeling, and every moment. Studies have shown that moderate physical activity can increase circulating serotonin, the molecule involved with modulating mood and cognition, as well as norepinephrine, the chemical associated with learning and focus. These increased levels of neurotransmitters help the brain process information more efficiently. They also bolster your mood. (It's likely you are familiar with serotonin already—it's the neurotransmitter that popular antidepression medications, selective serotonin reuptake inhibitors [SSRIs], work upon.)

Finally, research studies have shown that exercise can significantly increase brain-growth factors like brain-derived neurotrophic factor. BDNF is often referred to as brain fertilizer, and for good reason. This molecule is directly linked to brain growth—and explains why Gage saw the effects he did in his running mice.

Myokine Signaling

As scientists have gained the tools to look deeper into *how* moving your body can lead to the release of all these different molecules in the brain, they've discovered a unique means of muscle-to-brain signaling. Every time you contract your muscles, they release special molecules called myokines. Myokines are cytokines, or small proteins that help control inflammation in the body. These bad boys not only help protect the muscles from degeneration as you age, they also talk to other organs, like the brain, to increase BDNF and, consequently, improve cognition.

TALLYING UP THE BENEFITS

When you put all these fascinating studies together, it becomes clear that exercise kicks off a wide range of molecular events that help to keep the brain in tip-top shape, promoting Mental Fitness. Studies have even shown, repeatedly, that a regular exercise routine is a viable treatment option for depression, chronic stress, and anxiety. In a landmark clinical trial, James Blumenthal, PhD, a researcher at Duke University, compared regular exercise to Zoloft, a commonly prescribed antidepressant medication, in patients who had been diagnosed with major depressive disorder. He and his colleagues discovered, much to their surprise, that patients assigned to the exercise condition improved just as much as those who were prescribed the drug. When the researchers followed up a year later, study participants who continued to regularly exercise were much more likely to achieve remission from their depressive symptoms.

Years later, when Blumenthal expanded the trial, he discovered similar results in depressed adults who also had anxiety symptoms. Exercise eased those symptoms for study participants—leading him to suggest that exercise should augment, and can sometimes replace, pharmacotherapy in the treatment of both these rampant mental health conditions.

We see why, on the biological side of things, physical activity can literally open up the pathways and neural connections linked to stress reduction and improved mood. It does so through the release of important neuromodulatory molecules like endorphins, neurotransmitters, growth factors, and myokines. But exercise has also been shown to provide powerful psychological benefits to those who regularly engage. In a 2022 study, researchers examined how developing a regular exercise routine resulted in patients acknowledging a greater sense of self-efficacy and self-esteem. The act of doing—or, in this specific case, moving—helped to create a fundamental shift in how people view their own ability to change their circumstances and exhibit agency over their own lives. Movement helped provide distraction from negative thoughts. It boosted self-confidence. And it improved people's perceptions of their own self-image.

Exercise can also work as a preventative measure for mental health symptoms, as well as neurodegenerative disease. A large meta-analysis, which included hundreds of thousands of people to more fully understand the link between activity and depression, found that moving your body could help keep your mood up. The authors simply concluded, "Increasing evidence shows that physical activity is associated with reduced risk for depression, pointing to a potentially modifiable target for prevention." Carl Cotman, PhD, a neuroscientist at the University of California, Irvine's Institute for Brain Aging and Dementia, was one of the first researchers to demonstrate that exercise increases BDNF in animal models. Those studies also showed that exercise was associated with reduced amyloid-beta plaques, the sticky tangled proteins that are believed to cause memory impairment in Alzheimer's disease. But what might be even more fascinating about Cotman's work is that he showed that these beneficial effects last a week beyond a single workout. The workout you do today can still provide brain-boosting effects tomorrow—and up to a week after, too. Other studies have shown similar effects when it comes to dementia and Parkinson's disease.

While we are only in the infancy of understanding the many ways exercise can benefit the brain, it's clear that movement does a body good. Exercise helps the brain to grow, change, and adapt. More importantly, it doesn't take a marathon or a century ride to reap the benefits.

OKAY, BUT HOW MUCH IS ENOUGH?

This is the million-dollar question. And ever since Rusty Gage noticed that brain volume increases in running mice, scientists have sought to quantify the right dosage of exercise for maximum brain benefits. While the CDC recommends 150 minutes of aerobic exercise per week, it's not exactly a specific recommendation. One hundred fifty minutes of what kind of activity? At what intensity? I have more than a few patients who tell me that they'll start exercising when I can give them an exact prescription for what will help their brains most.

Certainly, over the past few decades, physicians and sports physiologists have looked for the optimal exercise recipe. But they haven't been able to come up with one. Studies that look at running, walking, strength training, yoga, and just about any other exercise you can think of show some benefit. In 2018, researchers from Harvard Medical School conducted a systematic review of nearly one hundred independent studies in hopes of coming up with the appropriate exercise dose. After careful analysis, they concluded that at least fifty-two hours over a twenty-five-week period—so about two hours per week—seemed to be the baseline to improve cognitive performance in older adults. But they also added that they "found no relationships between cognitive improvements and session time, exercise frequency, intensity, and weekly minutes." A more recent meta-analysis found moderate reductions in depressive symptoms in exercises ranging from jogging to tai chi, with effects proportional to exercise intensity.

This is good news. Because it means your mileage is going to—and is supposed to—vary. To heal the modern brain, you don't have to keep your heart in the max zone for ten minutes at a time. You don't have to take an hourlong class when your schedule can only accommodate twenty minutes. You don't have to embrace pain. And you don't ever have to spend time doing a physical activity that you hate. You can do what you enjoy and build up intensity as you go.

Another study, out of Australia, suggests that structured dance may be your best bet for healing the modern brain. In this systematic review, the researchers looked at everything from ballet to line-dancing interventions to improve both physical and psychological health. They learned that people who engage in dance show higher scores on measures of psychological and cognitive outcomes, including metrics that look at depression, motivation, and memory. They argue that dance may have an edge over other exercises because it often has a strong social element to it—and because learning choreography challenges the mind as well as the body.

But that doesn't mean you need to go out and immediately buy yourself some tap shoes. We all inhabit different bodies, with different experiences and needs. There isn't going to be a one-size-fits-all answer when it comes to the best form of physical exercise. There shouldn't be. We should all be finding physical activities that work for us instead of against us. We should find ways to move our body with love and joy. As you read those words, it's possible you are still asking, "Okay, but what *should* I do?" I would reply with a more important question: "What would you *like* to do?"

REDEFINING OUR RELATIONSHIP WITH MOVEMENT

When Ramona, a middle-aged corporate executive, first started coming to see me, she was quite unhappy with her life. She was single and unsatisfied in her job but felt like she couldn't make any moves to change her life for the better. She was, for lack of a better word, stuck. Each day, she'd go into the office and put in her eight hours. Then she'd go home and sit in front of the television until she fell asleep, usually on the couch.

"Have you thought about looking for a new job?" I asked.

"What's the point? They're all going to be the same. Nothing would change for me except which subway stop I get off at," she replied.

I had been encouraging her to try new activities for a while—mostly in hopes that she'd make some new friends or even meet a potential significant other. She was equally resistant to that idea.

"I'm so tired at the end of the day, I wouldn't be any fun," she said. "I can't think of anything I really want to try anyway."

A few months later, during our monthly check-in, she looked buoyant. Something had changed for her—but I wasn't sure what.

"Tell me what's going on with you," I said.

"I started dancing again," she said.

Dancing? Never once, in all of our time together, had she ever mentioned dancing. Anytime I mentioned the possibility of adding some physical activity to her schedule, she made it clear that she just wasn't "the active type."

"I used to dance the tango when I was younger," she said. "I really enjoyed it, but I just fell out of the habit. Then, last month, I saw an ad for a tango night not far from my apartment. I just went for it."

By the next time we spoke, she was going out to tango-dance a couple of nights a week. She would meet some new friends who kept her apprised of the different tango events around town. It was the most energized I'd ever seen her.

"It's so much fun. I go and I end up dancing for two hours straight," she said. "I didn't know I had it in me anymore!"

"Well, regular exercise can work wonders on mood and motivation," I said.

"It doesn't feel like exercise to me. It's just fun," said Ramona.

I remember thinking, in the moment, that even if she had taken up my advice to go to the gym or start walking to increase her physical activity, dancing the tango offered her so much more. Her brain was still benefiting from the increased blood flow and heightened release of neuromodulatory molecules. But her mood and outlook were also bolstered by the fact that dancing brought her so much joy. Win-win.

That's why it's so important, when it comes to physical activity, to consider what you like to do. So often, we think about exercise in ways that are detrimental to our well-being. We are so worried about hitting certain metrics—usually shrinking our waistlines—we don't see the simple joy that can come from moving your body. Exercise instead becomes a chore, not something that fuels us and engages us.

There are so many movements that can help improve your Mental Fitness. You may know that physical activities are broadly categorized as either open-skill or closed-skill exercises. Running, swimming, and stationary bike riding fall into the closed-skill group. They take place in a predictable and static environment—and the movements themselves are repetitive in nature with expected outcomes. Open-skill activities, however, are done in a more dynamic environment. Things change—and you have to adapt and respond. Team sports are open-skill exercises. As are rock climbing, dancing, and pickleball. And while Gage's mice saw brain benefits from running, other studies suggest that open-skill activities might provide your brain an even bigger boost.

That includes badminton. Yep, you heard me correctly. Badminton. Researchers at National Taiwan University compared BDNF production—remember, that "brain fertilizer" we talked about earlier—in students who spent thirty minutes running and those who spent the same amount of time playing badminton. They discovered that study participants in the badminton condition produced more BDNF than their running counterparts. I'm not saying that this means you should take up badminton (after all, all the courts have been taken over by the pickleball enthusiasts). What I am saying is that our narrow definitions of traditional aerobic exercise must be expanded. The pool of options available to you is much bigger than you think. Even basic stretching has been shown to increase serotonin and reduce feelings of anxiety. Everyone, no matter who you are or what your current fitness level is, can benefit from incorporating more movement into their lives.

EMBRACING JOYFUL MOVEMENT

Each morning, at exactly six thirty, the people of Japan take part in a shared experience of movement. Radio calisthenics are broadcast to homes, businesses, schools, and parks. These free sessions provide a daily guided-exercise routine designed to encourage stretching and light aerobic activity. And with over twenty-seven million people listening in and moving along, it's not just a token gesture. It's a normal, daily practice in the nation with the highest life expectancy in the world. Schoolchildren, salarymen, mothers, retirees, and others all make time to start their day with the shared experience of movement.

I'm not saying that you need to tune in and join them—although, if you are in the same time zone, it wouldn't hurt! What I am saying is that a large part of healing the modern brain and making it more resilient in the face of stress is finding ways to regularly move your body. Changing your outlook, as well as your habits, surrounding movement is a fundamental piece of achieving Mental Fitness.

Today, when I talk to my patients about the importance of physical activity, I try to leave the dreaded E-word (exercise) out of it. I've learned it's better for many to think of the daily recommendations in terms of movement, or even play. So, as you think about the daily recommendations for physical activity and how to incorporate them into your own life, I recommend choosing activities based on your own preferences, likes, dislikes, and circumstances. Forget a specific prescription. Do what works for you.

It's time to adopt a new mindset about movement. As we work to achieve Mental Fitness, we need to think beyond "exercise" and make sure we are receiving what we need from the physical activities we choose to bring into our lives. When you can take pleasure in movement, you'll find the time, like Ramona, to do it regularly. As you build these new activity habits, you'll quickly see that you are providing your brain with the things it needs to stay healthy, resilient, and mentally fit. That is, ultimately, what will lead to greater life satisfaction, improved mental clarity, and a positive mood.

CHAPTER 6

Sleep

Noah had always been a go-getter. He came to me after experiencing some minor panic attacks in college. Since graduation, he had been managing his anxiety and, by all accounts, thriving. He had taken a role as an analyst at a large financial services company and was making a name for himself. He is exactly the kind of person that these kinds of high-end firms love: smart, personable, hard-working, and eager to please. Within a few months at his new job, he was fast-tracked for promotion. He was then asked to oversee the small but critical merger of two Swiss companies. That's when things started to fall apart.

Thanks to the six-hour time difference between New York City and Geneva, within only a few weeks Noah started experiencing serious disruptions to his sleep. Every night, starting at 2:00 a.m., the work calls and emails from his European counterparts would start rolling in. And given Noah's work ethic and his desire to shine in his new role, he felt like he couldn't wait to deal with those communications until the beginning of his own workday. Instead he would haul himself out of bed and respond immediately. By the time he finished handling the influx, it would be time to get up and head into the office.

Within a few weeks, Noah's mood took a serious downturn. He was exhausted all the time. An avid runner and gym goer, he started skipping workouts to try to keep up with work. But his mental state also changed. He started to feel anxious about the emails he was receiving from his colleagues. He felt like they weren't being completely forthcoming about important information that would affect the merger. He was compelled to start double-checking and even redoing others' work. He started smoking again after quitting several years earlier, and his alcohol intake was way up, too. In addition, he started to experience some paranoia, believing that some of his coworkers might even be trying to pull him from the Switzerland deal. Then his panic attacks returned.

As someone who met with Noah every week, I was shocked to see how quickly he had deteriorated in such a short amount of time. The tools we had been using to help him with his anxiety weren't working for him anymore. Realizing something more was going on with him, I asked him how he was sleeping.

"Oh, I'm getting maybe a couple hours a night," he told me. "It's hard to go to sleep without a couple of drinks. And when I do sleep, I can only sleep for an hour, maybe two. I just can't seem to turn off my brain long enough to sleep any longer than that."

His answer alarmed me. I quickly realized that if we couldn't find a way to help Noah get some sleep, he would continue to decline to the point where he'd likely need hospitalization. When you don't get enough sleep over an extended period of time, a vicious cycle starts. Without the restorative power of rest, Noah's anxiety and paranoia would continue to grow. His depression would deepen and eventually lead to issues with thinking and processing. Those issues would proliferate, leading to a psychiatric crisis. I've seen it more times than I care to count.

While Noah believed he was just doing what was required to excel at work, the truth was he was doing himself lasting harm. For far too long, scientists and medical professionals didn't understand the true purpose of sleep. We had an idea it was important, but we didn't grasp just how fundamental it was to our overall health and well-being. Today we understand that sleep offers us more than just mere rest. It plays a pivotal role in the daily upkeep of our physical and mental health.

And while the world may often ask us to forgo a good night's sleep to keep up with work, school, or family, let's face it: the ability to skip sleep to achieve is too often worn like a badge of honor. Deprioritizing healthy sleep is one of the worst things we can do for our mental health as we attempt to juggle the overwhelming demands of modern life.

YOUR BRAIN ON SLEEP

In 1959, New York City's top radio personality, Peter Tripp, had an interesting idea. To help raise money for the March of Dimes—and, of course, to drum up some publicity for himself—he announced his intention to break a world record by staying awake for eight straight days, or two hundred hours. To add a little extra oomph to the stunt, he said he would broadcast his radio show from his booth in Times Square for the entire time. Listeners were encouraged not only to listen, but to pledge money to the charity based on the amount of time he could stay awake.

Given the risks involved with such an endeavor, Tripp's radio station engaged local sleep researchers to monitor him over his eight-day stint. They were there not only to make sure he wasn't in physical danger (nudging him as needed and providing stimulants to help him stay awake), but also to test his cognitive skills over his pledged time. Tripp began the experiment in good spirits, but as the hours and days wore on, the researchers noted the popular deejay was experiencing severe physical and mental symptoms. Somehow he was able to keep his show going over the course of the eight days. Yet, when he was off the air, researchers observed that Tripp's mood changed drastically. He was incredibly irritable and terse. About one hundred hours in, Tripp's capacity for words and his memory—both skills that helped him become the radio success he was—began to fail him. Twenty hours later, he reported hallucinations as his tether to reality became more and more tenuous, and he even started to believe that the researchers were trying to frame him for a crime.

Tripp managed to achieve his goal mostly thanks to the help of some powerful stimulants in those last hours. But the experience was not without consequence. After twenty-four hours of rest, the experts told the world that Tripp had experienced no lasting damage from his eight days of wakefulness. Alas, friends and family would report that he was never quite the same. He experienced mood swings, anxiety, and forgetfulness for the rest of his life.

If you've ever pulled an all-nighter or two, you are probably familiar with the early symptoms of sleep deprivation. Even when we just experience disrupted sleep, thanks to a colicky baby or a loud neighbor, our cognitive function suffers the next day. We are tired and have trouble focusing. It's not easy to learn or retain new information. Finding words—or remembering all the items on our to-do list—can be a chore. And our mood and motivation levels suffer.

Is it any wonder that sleep and mental health are intimately linked? It's no coincidence that you'll find chronic sleep issues listed as a symptom for the vast majority of diagnosable mental health disorders. It is particularly prevalent in patients with anxiety, depression, bipolar disorder, and attention-deficit hyperactivity disorder.

Tripp's story is an extreme one, but the reality is that most of us don't give sleep the attention it deserves. Sadly, millions of people suffer every day from too little or poor-quality sleep. They all almost certainly experience some degree of impact on their mental health and brain health. Noah, for one, was suffering a great deal thanks to his own lack of sleep.

As you read this and reflect on your own experiences with poor sleep, you may ask yourself just *why* sleep has such an impact. The truth of the matter is, for decades, scientists weren't entirely sure, either. They knew that sleeping is required for every single person. Most species experience this kind of profound change in consciousness in a cyclical way—even insects. But, for far too long, we haven't understood what sleep is, what it does, how it affects our brains, or even what constitutes "good" sleep. Thankfully, the new science of sleep is continuing to open our eyes to sleep's purpose and why sleep deprivation can wreak such havoc on our thoughts, feelings, and behaviors. Studies now agree that banking eight hours of quality shut-eye can help regulate mood, facilitate memory and learning, and allow the brain to do some internal housekeeping work. But before we delve into that, it's important to understand the basics of how sleep affects our bodies and brains.

SLEEP: THE BASICS

What happens when you drift off to la-la land each night? Your body undergoes a remarkable transformation. Your breathing slows. Your temperature, heart rate, and blood pressure drop. Your muscles relax. Your metabolism undergoes profound changes. You lose consciousness and your senses are inhibited. Once you transition into sleep, you are, essentially, uncoupled from the busy, outside world.

Nearly every organ in your body is affected in one way or another, including your brain. Your brain's activity changes, decelerating into slow, coordinated waves. We often talk about sleep as a time of rest, yet we now understand the brain is not switched off and resetting things. Rather, it is hard at work, helping us to consolidate and store the important information we learned during the day without the distractions of new sensory inputs coming in. Seven to nine hours a night of sleep (a bit more for teenagers) brings with it restoration, rejuvenation, and good health.

It's important to understand that sleep is not a single, monolithic entity. Instead, it's a process that contains distinct stages—each with its own functions. We cycle through these different stages throughout the night, on repeat, to receive the most benefit from our slumber.

There are two main types of sleep: rapid eye movement (REM) sleep and non-REM (NREM) sleep. REM sleep earned its name from what outsiders can observe: your eyes begin to shift and flick in different directions during this type of sleep. In this stage, your heart rate and breathing increase and you begin to dream. The brain is more active during REM sleep, too, showing activity that is much more similar to that which occurs in a waking mind.

With NREM sleep, however, the eyes do not show these distinct eye movements. Many call this type of sleep "deep" or "slow wave" sleep. That's because brain activity is dampened during the last two stages of NREM. And, as researchers recently learned, those slow waves are part of what is required for the brain to keep itself clean and healthy.

But back to the stages. After you fall asleep, the first cycle you experience is NREM sleep. It's when you are just starting to fall asleep, hovering between drowsy consciousness and complete lights-out. You can think of this first stage as your body's way of powering the brain down to bring you into a deep, restful state. The next stage, also NREM sleep, is known as light sleep. Here your heart rate and breathing start to slow. This is where you lose consciousness, but it would still be fairly easy for a loud noise or a partner stealing your covers to wake you. The final two stages of NREM sleep are that deep or slow-wave sleep I just mentioned. Brain activity will take on that distinct, slow wavelike rhythm and you are much harder to wake as you cycle through this type of sleep. Thanks to recent advances in neuroscience, we now understand that special rhythm allows the brain to store and reorganize new information, as well as do some important cleanup work. More on that in a bit.

After you go through the four stages of NREM sleep, you'll cycle into REM. While your eyes may be moving fast, the rest of your body is not moving at all. Your muscles are inactive—you are, for all intents and purposes, paralyzed. I know that might sound a little scary, but the alternative is scarier. You want your body's motor activity on pause during REM sleep. Not only does it allow your body time to rest and do some repair work, but it also stops you from acting out your dreams, which occur during the REM cycle. There's a medical condition called REM sleep behavior disorder (RBD), which can be caused by brain degeneration and some medications, that does not render your motor system inactive. This can lead to sleepwalking or other issues. Comedian Mike Birbiglia, who has been diagnosed with RBD, recounted in one of his stand-up routines how he threw himself through a closed second-floor window in a hotel during a particularly menacing dream. It's a funny bit, but also quite terrifying. It demonstrates the danger of your body being able to move as you experience your dreams. You don't want to literally start running, with no awareness of the outside world, when you dream of being chased by some weird monster or start punching some imaginary foe when you are lying in bed next to your spouse or children.

Across a single night, over eight hours of uninterrupted sleep, you can expect to cycle through the four stages of NREM, followed by REM sleep, four to five times. With each successive cycle, you'll spend less time in those last two NREM stages of deep sleep.

You may be wondering why I took you through all these stages. It's because sleep is not just one thing. There's a lot happening in the brain and body during the sleep cycle. And given that we spend almost one-third of our total lives sleeping, and the negative effects sleep deprivation has on almost every bodily system, it's important to understand that. Each of these distinct physiological stages plays a significant role in both physical and mental health. In some ways, sleep, like the brain, is one of the final frontiers of human medicine. We still don't know the entirety of what sleep does across these different phases, but thanks to recent advances in our understanding of sleep's function, we now see these tightly choreographed stages of sleep play a pivotal role in promoting brain plasticity, dampening excess inflammation, and regulating immune function. And all three are vital to maintaining overall brain health.

SLEEP AND NEUROPLASTICITY

Have you ever had a conversation with a friend and found yourself unable to come up with the name of a song or a movie—only to wake up with the title front of mind the next day? It's a fairly common phenomenon. And this seemingly random recall is because one of sleep's functions is to help us learn and remember.

You've already heard me talk about the importance of grow mode. When the brain is obtaining what it needs, it can facilitate neuroplasticity, or the natural ability to rewire itself to help you better adapt to the world around you. When your brain can make strong new synaptic connections, it is optimized to process all the sensory information coming in and determine the appropriate decisions and behaviors to help you best respond to it. Being in grow mode is also preventative, producing important neurochemicals that can help your brain protect itself against the negative processes we see occurring in mood and other mental health disorders.

Scientists have long known that sleep greatly affects the hippocampus, better known as the memory center of the brain. In a controlled study on sleep habits, researchers observed healthy activity in the hippocampus in those who received the recommended eight hours of quality sleep the night before. Those who went without it showed much worse readings. Things weren't working as they should.

That difference can be chalked up to a process called memory consolidation. Simply put, it's the brain reshelving the books, so to speak, so we can remember what we've previously learned and easily access it in the brain's long-term memory vault. During slow-wave sleep, our brain cells take on a unique pattern of activity. Jan Born, a sleep researcher from Germany's University of Tübingen, was able to demonstrate in animal models that this specific pattern of activity helps us reactivate and reorganize the things we learned during the day so they can be consolidated and placed into long-term-memory storage.

Dozens upon dozens of psychological studies have shown that most animal species, including humans, do better on memory tasks after a good night's rest. It doesn't matter if you are studying for your organic chemistry final, learning some funky dance steps, or trying to remember the words of a new language—you will show better recall if you are tested on the information after cycling through slow-wave sleep.

Something else is happening in the brain as we slumber: it prioritizes what we remember. Consider all the information that your senses pick up during the day. There's no need for you to remember it all and, frankly, from a simple cost-benefit perspective, it doesn't make sense for you to do so. It would be learning overdrive and, over time, the brain would be unable to manage all that excess and unnecessary information.

To find balance, the brain takes stock of all the synapses in the brain during sleep. Researchers Giulio Tononi and Chiara Cirelli, at the University of Wisconsin–Madison's Center for Sleep and Consciousness, have demonstrated that, during deep sleep, the brain undergoes what they call "synaptic homeostasis." That is, the strength of synaptic connections, on the whole, decreases while we rest. This allows the brain to remove unnecessary data to better prepare the brain for learning the next day. It's an essential process for keeping the brain in grow mode.

It probably comes as no surprise that when you skip sleep, both memory consolidation and synaptic homeostasis are affected. Lack of sleep interferes with these key, internal processes that help keep the brain healthy, fit, and ready to make new synaptic connections.

Sleep is essential to move the brain into grow mode and, as a result, an integral part of strong mental health.

SLEEP AND INFLAMMATION

Let's talk inflammation—the first line of defense for your body's immune system. Inflammation, in small doses, is a good thing. It's the immune system's way of dealing with illness or injuries. Immune cells come to the damaged area of the body, clean up any damaged cells, and promote healing. The problem is when inflammation becomes chronic. Unfortunately, the medical community is still very much in the dark as to why, at times, the immune system doesn't know when to say "when" and continues to send immune cells to previously injured areas with a cleanup mission. If it isn't addressed, that chronic inflammation can lead to inadvertent damage to healthy cells and tissues. It's a big problem, especially in the brain, where important neural circuits can be damaged. That's why, when it comes to a healthy brain, you want to avoid excess inflammation as much as possible.

The brain not only consumes approximately twenty percent of the body's total energy costs—much, much more than any other organ—it also generates a fair amount of waste from our neurons as they facilitate thinking, feeling, and doing from day to day. Experts estimate our brain cells produce seven grams of waste every single day. That's one and a half teaspoons of trash, made up of the by-products of cellular respiration like carbon dioxide, water, ammonia, and various proteins, which our three-pound brains have to somehow flush out. It's imperative that they do so. Otherwise that debris can interfere with healthy functioning. Proteins in particular can gum up the works, making it harder for neurons to send signals to their neighbors to support efficient processing. In extreme cases, this waste can lead to neurodegenerative disorders. In Alzheimer's and Parkinson's disease, for example, proteins like amyloid beta and tau are not cleared from the brain. Over time, they form sticky plaques that lead to memory issues, slower cognitive processing, and movement problems.

Until fairly recently, scientists had no idea how the brain dealt with its waste. The body has a sophisticated network of vessels and nodes that work as a waste-removal system. It's called the lymphatic system—and it uses lymph, a unique fluid, to carry toxins and other debris out of the body. Without it our organs would be unable to stay healthy and function properly. Yet, funnily enough, up until the last decade, there was no physiological evidence that the brain or spinal cord was connected to this system. Given that the brain has such high energy needs and produces so much extra waste, many wondered how exactly the brain was doing all that necessary housekeeping. It was a big mystery.

Maiken Nedergaard, a neuroscientist at the University of Rochester Medical Center, did not think the brain was an exception—it would, like the kidney or lung, need some way to handle waste removal. After all, all bodily organs need a way to take out the trash, even if the brain's way isn't readily apparent. Dr. Nedergaard and her colleagues hypothesized that glial cells, a key part of the brain's support crew, must be involved. It wasn't until Nedergaard started monitoring the brains of rodents as they slept that she finally found the evidence she needed to prove her hypothesis correct.

The Rochester scientists discovered that sleep rearranged the brain cells. Under the microscope, the cells appeared to become smaller, almost shrinking into themselves, to make the spaces between them bigger. After making that extra room, astrocytes, a star-shaped type of glial cell, move through the brain, creating a network of canals and conduits throughout the organ, allowing cerebral-spinal fluid (CSF) to flow through it. This free-flowing CSF cleans out the troublesome debris, moving it out past the blood-brain barrier and into the lymphatic system. It's a bit like hosing off your stoop to drive any dirt toward the municipal sewer system.

This study finally solved the mystery of how the brain handled its housekeeping duties. The researchers called it the glial-dependent lymphatic transport system and quickly shortened it to the "glymphatic system," a fun play on the words "glial" and "lymphatic."

This macroscopic waste-clearance system allows your brain to be thoroughly cleansed while you sleep. It removes waste metabolites, proteins, and other neurotoxic waste materials—the buildup of which can lead to excess and chronic inflammation in the brain—while simultaneously distributing essential minerals, fats, amino acids, and glucose that help to support neural health.

Think of your brain like an office building. Each day, the essential functions of the office create trash. Whiteboards are written on. Papers are moved around. It's only at night, after everyone has gone home, that the cleaning crew can empty wastebaskets, organize papers, and make sure everything is put back into working, productive order. That's exactly what happens to your brain during sleep.

This new understanding of the brain's waste-clearance system has fundamentally changed the ways we think about sleep, its importance, and the consequences of not getting enough of it. Sleep is a prerequisite for this waste system to function properly. When we don't sleep, over time, the brain's extra waste builds up—leading to increased, even chronic inflammation. Now that we understand that chronic inflammation in the brain is associated with depression, anxiety, neurodegeneration, and other brain health issues, the importance of sleep and waste removal cannot be understated. It's just one of the reasons why sleep has become a new frontier in our understanding of how to optimize brain health and recovery.

SLEEP AND THE MICROBIOME

You probably wouldn't be surprised to hear that the length and quality of our sleep also affect how well our immune system functions. Multiple studies have shown that those who get only four hours of sleep a night will see as much as a seventy-percent reduction in crucial immune cells. The reasons for this remain somewhat of a mystery: the human immune system is very complex. Yet many experts hypothesize that lack of sleep leads to immune suppression. The system simply doesn't have the ability to create as many infection- and injury-fighting cells. Others suggest that sleep deprivation, which comes with a rise in a stress hormone called cortisol, may interfere with immunity. While biologists are still trying to understand all the ins and outs of how sleep influences our immune system, the end result is the same: when we don't sleep well, our immune system is hamstrung. Sleep-deprived individuals will have more difficulty fighting off foreign invaders than their well-rested counterparts.

But sleep deprivation also impacts the composition of the microbiome, or the trillions of bacteria that live within our gastrointestinal systems. You see, the bacteria that make their homes in our gut aren't just there to help us digest our dinners. They can send important signals to the hundreds of millions of neurons that line the gastrointestinal tract, sending a direct line to the brain. Have you ever wondered why people with anxiety often have corresponding GI issues? As their stress level goes up, so do their trips to the bathroom. People living with depression often aren't hungry—or, alternatively, are eating far too much. Gut issues and mental health issues go hand in hand.

That's because the gut and brain are in almost constant communication, through an important circuit called the gut-brain axis. If you think about it, we, as a species, instinctively know the two are related. We often talk about our "gut feelings" or how we feel "gutted" when something bad happens. When we are anxious, we often feel nauseated—or the fluttering of stomach butterflies. This crucial signaling pathway between the gut and brain provides a strong evolutionary advantage. Since the brain is an energy hog, and our energy needs are met by the foods we eat, they should be talking. The brain tells us when we need more food—or if we've eaten far too much.

The gut also happens to be the largest endocrine organ in the body. It secretes important hormones that help to mediate our immune response. As it extends from the mouth to anus, it can keep tabs on all of the bodily organs, making sure everything is in full working order. When it's not, it can release immune cells and pro-inflammatory molecules to help deal with any issues. And the microbiome, the trillions of microorganisms that reside there, help to keep the lines of communication between the gut and the brain open.

Simply stated, you want a diverse microbiome with plenty of different species of bacteria to help maintain these communication channels. When there is a lack of diversity, those signaling lines break down. The body may send far too many immune cells to the brain, leading to excess inflammation. That's why study after study has found that a lack of diversity in the microbiome is linked to issues with mood, cognition, and an individual's overall risk of mental illness. Studies have even shown that when you can increase that diversity, improving the overall composition of the gut bacteria, through diet or supplementation, you can improve or even relieve depressive and anxiety symptoms.

The latest research, however, shows that foods are not the only way to influence the microbiome. As it turns out, lack of sleep can lead to decreased diversity in your gut bacteria. The reasons why are not entirely clear. Many experts hypothesize that lack of sleep, which often leads to an increase in cortisol, a stress hormone, works to kill off certain gut bacteria species. Yet, regardless of the exact mechanism, researchers who have examined the relationship between poor sleep and the microbiome have observed that sleep issues can trigger the gut to ramp up immune cell release, which ultimately leads to increased neuroinflammation. As we've already discussed, this can up your risk for cognitive impairment, depression, and anxiety. It's just another way that sleep can impact our mental health.

IT'S TIME TO THINK ABOUT SLEEP HYGIENE

Given the relationship between sleep and neuroplasticity, inflammation, and the microbiome, it's no wonder a lack of sleep has myriad effects on our Mental Fitness. It plays a key role in archiving the experiences we have during the day, transforming our short-term memories into long-term ones. Sleep helps put your brain into grow mode, while cleaning out brain debris. It can also help ensure that you maintain a diverse and healthy microbiome.

It's time for a fundamental shift in how we think about sleep. For too long, we've romanticized sleep deprivation. We've cheered on the student staying up all night to cram for the big final or the office worker burning the candle at both ends to make themselves ready for that big client meeting. We have given the "I'll sleep when I'm dead" crowd far too much adulation. Especially since we now know that this worshipful dedication to poor sleep is actually fostering a culture of brain fog, exhaustion, poor mood, and long-term mental health symptoms. It's time to change the conversation and talk more about how to improve sleep.

When I was training as a psychiatrist, I remember one of my mentors telling me, "The most dangerous thing is a man who is not sleeping." He said when a patient came to the hospital and there was a history of ongoing sleep deprivation, you had to immediately take the possibility of suicidal ideation and psychosis into account.

"If your patient is not sleeping," he told us young residents, "you should not be sleeping."

Now that we know more about the function of sleep, his words seem even more poignant. And it was his voice that came to mind when Noah first told me about his sleep issues. I quickly understood that we needed to address his sleep issues immediately, before things got worse for him. The big question: How?

Historically, medicine, including psychiatry, treats sleep issues quite bluntly. We tend to handle it by whipping out our prescription pads. Benzodiazepines. Trazodone. Zolpidem. Ramelteon. These prescription drugs all work in different ways, and they help many people fall and stay asleep each night. Roughly one in five people regularly take some sort of sleep aid—and that number increases to one in three for older demographics. The reality is that people rely on these medications because they often work and the side effects are more desirable than sleep deprivation. Yet use of these medications doesn't come without a cost. Often people become dependent on these sleep aids.

I have many patients who depend on sleep medications. And they can be helpful—at least for a time. I don't want to add to the stigma of using sleep meds, especially when they are called for. Yet, as new research comes in, it's become clear that a medicated sleep isn't necessarily the best option for helping people achieve what their brains need from sleep. Too often, the quality of medication-assisted sleep just isn't the same as naturally induced slumber. You don't hit the same stages of sleep—nor do you spend as much time in them. And with the risk of addiction, it's becoming more and more clear that medicated sleep shouldn't be the go-to option. To really make a difference, we need to understand *why* people struggle to fall asleep. Then we can find a way to make positive changes so that people can heal their brains—and move on with their lives.

That's where sleep hygiene comes in.

You might think of it as a nighttime routine or a bedtime ritual. I often refer to it as "embracing the wind-down." But sleep hygiene, simply defined, is the collection of habits, choices, and environmental factors that dictate the quality, ease, and consistency of your sleep. These are the variables over which each of us has some control. Yet, for far too many of us, suboptimal routines that interfere with healthy sleep have become ingrained. But most people, by making just a few simple changes, will see a massive improvement in the quality of their sleep—and as a result, improved mental health and fitness.

What do these changes look like? Well, this varies from person to person and may even change over time, depending on what's happening in your life. Together we will identify what changes will work best for you. Then you can engage in positive habits that will help you fall and stay asleep each night, and the quality of your sleep will improve. More importantly, these essential benefits from sleep will support brain health and Mental Fitness.

NEXT UP, THE DREAM FACTOR

One of my favorite things to do with patients is to ask them about their dreams. I usually do this in the first session—and it can lead to some very interesting (and quite therapeutic) conversations.

Sigmund Freud, the infamous nineteenth-century psychoanalyst, argued that dreams are "the royal road to a knowledge of the unconscious activities of the mind." Most psychology students are handed a copy of his seminal work, *The Interpretation of Dreams*, and think that the weird dream they had involving their fifth-grade teacher somehow represents some kind of repressed or unconscious fears or desires.

Luckily, new investigations into the function of dreaming show us that Freud's take may not be all it's cracked up to be. I'm not saying you don't have some things you need to work out regarding your elementary school experience—but your dream may represent something much more mundane. REM sleep, the type of sleep where we dream, may be setting the stage for memory consolidation.

Let me explain. Robert Stickgold, a Harvard University neuroscientist who has spent his career studying sleep, proposes that REM sleep offers our brains an opportunity to find connections between what we learned during the day and what is already present in our stored memory. His theory, called the Network Exploration to Understand Possibilities (NEXTUP), suggests that dream of your dentist may be there because he resembles someone else you know, and is already filed in your memory archives—or because his admonition to floss more reminded you of something else you've heard before. But, Stickgold contends, the idea is that dreams are all about loose connections. Hence his reference to understanding possibilities.

Studies looking at memory recall in participants who are awakened from REM sleep demonstrate that we are significantly more accurate at recalling loosely associated word pairs learned before sleeping when they are awakened during their REM cycles. For example, if study participants are asked to remember word pairs like "wrong and right" and "wrong and thief," they are better at remembering the latter after REM sleep and the former after deeper sleep stages.

That led Stickgold to hypothesize that REM sleep supports a hyperassociative state in the brain. To help determine what should be flagged and moved to long-term storage, the brain uses REM sleep to make these looser associations, building them out into a story of sorts, to see whether your brain has a strong emotional reaction to them. If it does, then those associations might be worth keeping around. Once you move into deep sleep, those associations are likely reevaluated, and, if they are deemed worthwhile, they are moved into long-term storage with the other learnings of the day.

What happens, though, when that deep-sleep evaluation period doesn't occur? You end up with a lot of associations that probably don't make a lot of sense. When you consider many of the symptoms that you commonly see in different mental health disorders, Stickgold's theory explains why so many individuals living with these disorders suffer from rumination, paranoia, and excess anxiety. They may be retaining associations that aren't always based in reality—and not holding on to the learning that would allow them to make better sense of the world around them. It quickly becomes apparent why a lack of deep sleep, where these more tenuous associations should be discarded, can lead to disordered thinking and other cognitive problems.

IDENTIFYING YOUR SLEEP DEMONS

The way we sleep is deeply tied to the way we live, so the best treatments are often rooted in the simple changes we make to our environment, schedule, and habits. Your sleep is a neglected piece of your mental health and Mental Fitness. When I started paying more attention to my sleep—monitoring it, actively engaging in ways to improve it, and changing my environment to make it more conducive to sleep—my sleep quality improved dramatically. That's why I think it's so important for you to start working to achieve a better night's sleep to bolster your mental health. I want you to start tonight.

The process of falling asleep, for many, is quite simple. They lie down. They close their eyes. And they are out like a light. For others, this process is anything *but* simple. One-third of the American population struggles with achieving sufficient rest. Those barriers create chronic fatigue and symptoms of mental health disorders. That's why it's so important to start by identifying your sleep demons. In doing so, you can create the restorative sleep your body and mind are craving.

The first step is to identify what may be interfering with your sleep. Take a few minutes to reflect on why you may have trouble sleeping. Do you have an uncomfortable mattress? Does your partner snore? Does the television keep you up later than you'd like? What is the temperature in your bedroom? It's possible that nothing immediately came to mind. That's okay. Your sleep demons may not be immediately obvious. If that's the case, reconsider the question when you go to bed tonight. What activities do you engage in before you try to sleep? What might be keeping you up at night? If you can fall asleep easily, but wake up periodically, try to identify what's waking you. Is it your bladder? Racing thoughts? Something else entirely? Leave a notebook by your bed and take note.

After talking with Noah, it was clear that the biggest issue affecting his sleep was the nighttime disruption from his Switzerland counterparts. He's not alone. A 2022 survey revealed that nearly two-thirds of Americans bring their phone to bed with them each night. But even if you don't spend an hour in bed scrolling through your social media feeds, the usage of tablets, computers, televisions, and other devices in the evening hours has been linked to reduced sleep quality and reduced levels of melatonin, the hormone that helps bring on that sleepy feeling. While scientists don't fully understand the lingering effects of blue screens on the eyes and the brain, we have known for a long time that bright lights, in general, are not conducive to good, quality sleep.

But, beyond the LED lights that power their screens, taking your phone—or any other device, for that matter—to bed with you creates other problems. Consider the activities you do on these devices. Maybe you play a game, check the game highlights, or scroll through headlines. Whatever it is, you are engaging in rapid-fire content that puts you in a stimulated, more anxious state.

In Noah's case, it was clear he was being overstimulated by all the emails coming in from Europe each night. He had to turn off those alerts. So, we made a plan for him to turn his notifications off after 10:00 p.m.—and to leave all of his devices, including his smart watch, outside the bedroom. Things could (and would have to) wait until morning.

Admittedly, at first Noah was resistant to this idea. He was afraid that he might miss something important from one of his European colleagues and get in trouble at work. By this point, however, he understood that he was standing at a precipice—and, thanks to his mental deterioration, was already making mistakes on the job. He agreed to try one week with his devices away from his bed as a test run. Not only did he quickly recognize that he wasn't going to lose his job if he didn't answer a 3:00 a.m. email, but he also saw how much his lack of sleep had been affecting him. After one night's uninterrupted rest, his mood and focus noticeably improved. After a few days, Noah reported he was back to feeling more like his old self. By the end of the week, he realized he hadn't had a single panic attack. He decided his devices would remain outside the bedroom.

Devices aren't the only sleep demon that may need to be reckoned with. When you go to bed and when you wake up are also important. Think about your nightly routine and when you wake up in the morning. The importance of a routine is often overlooked, particularly on days off from a work schedule. But sleep is governed by your internal body clock, and that kind of cyclical time mapping doesn't take time off. Experts, me included, recommend developing a nighttime sleep routine that works for you and then doing your best to stick to it, seven days a week. That means same bedtime, same wake time, day in and day out. It may seem extreme, but a consistent routine helps to let your body know when it's time to take rest. Here's where your phone can help with your sleep. Set an alarm at night to remind you it's time to start your winddown (and, of course, either power down your device, put it in sleep mode, or leave it outside the bedroom). Set an alarm clock in your room to wake you at the same time each morning. Within a few weeks, you'll see just how much a regular routine can improve the overall quality of your sleep each night.

As you think about your sleep demons, I also want you to consider the environment you create for sleeping. Check your five senses. Is the room dark? I mean, really dark? Think about it: For millennia, humans never had access to electricity or lights at night. We simply followed the day-night cycle and slept when the sun went down. Now, however, artificial lights are everywhere, wreaking havoc on our sleep physiology. Light exposure at the wrong times can alter your body's internal sleep clock, which, as you probably guessed, keeps your sleep-wake cycle out of rhythm, as darkness is correlated with increased melatonin production. Fade your lights down one to two hours before you go to bed. Invest in curtains—blackout or otherwise—to keep the bedroom dark. Or, if it's easier, buy an eye mask.

Listen to your surroundings and ask yourself, What helps me to relax? Is it silence, or do you prefer a little background noise? If the latter, consistent and ambient noise, like the sound generated from a white or pink noise machine, can be helpful for many who are looking to improve sleep conditions.

Have you considered your sense of smell? There have been eleven randomized, controlled tests showing a positive correlation between diffusing essential oils and improved sleep quality. It's not that there is necessarily anything mystically curative going on with the oils—it simply means that there's a clear connection between ambient scent, ambient noise, and healthy sleep. It gives your body and brain a signal that it's time to start preparing for rest.

Finally, I have to add a note on caffeine. I urge each of my patients to take a look at how much caffeine they're consuming throughout the day and when. Though it may seem like a harmless pick-me-up, most people don't realize that the caffeine in that 2:00 p.m. cup of coffee has a half-life of roughly six hours. Six hours! That means you will almost certainly still have plenty of caffeine in your system by the time you're winding down for bed at 9:00 or 10:00 p.m. I probably don't have to tell you that the stimulant properties of caffeine are the exact opposite of what you want when trying to accomplish restful, consistent, quality sleep.

Taking stock of your sleep demons isn't easy. I should know— during the pandemic, I started experiencing insomnia myself. I quickly realized that I really had no idea how much I was sleeping. As the old adage goes, you can't manage what you can't measure. It was only after I started wearing an Oura ring, a popular fitness and health tracker, that I realized just how off my sleep was. While larger watches or other devices that can measure sleep distracted me, having this small, unobtrusive ring on my finger was a great way to see how many hours I was getting a night—and then track my improvements as I started to address my own sleep demons. It made a huge difference and it's why I now suggest to my patients, including Noah, that they find a sleep tracker that will work for them.

Take a look at your own life at every stage of your day, and I imagine you'll begin to see the factors that are contributing to less-than-exceptional sleep. By identifying these, you can begin to make small changes that will have a massive impact on your overall brain health and mental health. Sleep is one of the most crucial factors in our quest to help you heal from depression and anxiety and take care of your modern brain.

SLEEP HYGIENE WORKSHEET

Assess your current sleep hygiene by answering the following questions:

1. What time do you go to bed each night?
   Monday:
   Tuesday:
   Wednesday:
   Thursday:
   Friday:
   Saturday:
   Sunday:

2. What time do you wake up each morning?
   Monday:
   Tuesday:
   Wednesday:
   Thursday:
   Friday:
   Saturday:
   Sunday:

3. What is your normal bedtime routine?

4. Describe your sleeping environment using your senses:
   What does it look like?
   What does it feel like?
   What does it sound like?
   What does it smell like?

5. How many hours before bed do you stop watching television or using your phone, tablet, or laptop?

6. Are you using a device (smart watch, Oura ring, or other) to monitor your sleep?

7. What time of day do you have your last caffeinated beverage?

8. How many alcoholic drinks do you have per night?

9. When do you last eat before bedtime?

10. Do you exercise, and if so, at what time of day?

11. What do you think about as you go to sleep?

Given what you've learned in this chapter, do any sleep demons jump out at you? Which ones?

Pick one sleep demon. What changes might you make to that aspect of your sleep hygiene to improve your sleep?

CHAPTER 7

Connection

Ronnie thought he had put his life back together quite well after his midlife divorce. He bought a house a few blocks away from the home he had previously shared with his ex-wife and teenage son. While he had gone on plenty of first and second dates, a new relationship hadn't blossomed from his efforts. His ex had met someone new fairly quickly after the divorce papers were signed, but Ronnie figured he had plenty of time to meet someone later. He had his career to think about—and, most importantly, figuring out how to be there for his son even if they were no longer sharing the same roof every night.

By the time his son was a junior in high school, dating became less and less of a priority. For all four years of his son's tenure in high school, you would find Ronnie in the stands at basketball games and track meets. Every other weekend, his son would stay at his house—and they'd usually hang out at home playing board games or head to the movies. His social life, such that it was, was deeply entwined with fatherhood. And while he didn't head out on his own all that often, when he did it was with other dads he met through his son's activities or with colleagues from work.

Then the bottom dropped out. When Ronnie's son left for college, the weekends that had once been filled with extracurricular activities (and the extra laundry that those activities always brought with it) were painfully empty. Right around the same time, Ronnie accepted a new job. The gig came with a significant pay raise—a nice perk for a guy who was now responsible for a hefty college tuition bill—but it also meant that he was now working in a new office with new people. He was having trouble connecting with his new colleagues. And trying to hang out with his old work buddies always seemed like an exercise in futility. They were always busy with their own families—or with their own job worries and complaints. By the time Ronnie came to see me, about six months later, he told me he was "not in a good place." After half an hour of conversation, it was clear that meant he was depressed and disconnected.

"I know it's natural to feel sad when your kid goes off to college," he told me. "But I'm gutted. I don't know what to do with myself. I come home from work and I'm by myself. I go out to eat, and I'm by myself. Saturday comes around, and I'm by myself. I see an ad for a movie and think, 'I'd like to see that,' and realize I can't think of anyone to ask to go with me. My ex-wife tells me I just need to make some new friends—but how do you even do that at my age?"

Ronnie, simply put, was lonely.

He's not alone. Vivek Murthy, surgeon general of the United States, raised the alarm about the growing epidemic of loneliness plaguing the United States. In 2023, he released a Surgeon General Advisory naming loneliness a public health crisis, noting that half of US adults report a significant degree of loneliness. This is important because our social connections play a crucial role in both our physical and mental health. Experts suggest that lacking social connection can increase the risk for premature death as much as being a regular cigarette smoker. It can also take a serious toll on one's mental health, with lonely people reporting more depression and anxiety symptoms.

Dr. Murthy's concerns affect those at every age, especially today, when people are more likely to move away from their extended families. They report having fewer friends as they grow older. And, like Ronnie, they often find themselves flustered at the thought of trying to figure out how to create new connections. (Yes. Sometimes Gen Z sounds like a divorced midlife dad.)

But it is important, because having strong social ties is an elusive and underutilized part of cultivating Mental Fitness.

FINDING REAL CONNECTION IN A HYPERCONNECTED WORLD

It seems like it should be fairly simple. What did your mom say to you when you went off to school or the playground as a kid: Have fun! Make a new friend!

But what used to just require a hello and shared affinity for the monkey bars becomes a little more complicated as we age. And, more and more, it seems like developing and maintaining connections is often easier said than done. I'm noticing, more and more, that people seem to be confused by what a healthy social connection really is—and how to best support those kinds of relationships.

Humans, by our very natures, are social creatures. Our brains are designed to promote social connection. Not only do they help us propagate the species, but they also ensure we have the help and support needed to survive. Back in the savanna, our hunter-gatherer ancestors relied on others to find food, avoid predators, and raise children. The whole idea of "it takes a village" was born from this idea. You need that village to take care of you during those times when maybe you can't take care of yourself. Community meant life. It was the key to our very survival—as individuals, and as a species.

We are a few millennia away from those old hunter-gatherer days. But the value of having a strong network still stands. And those networks are built from a range of different types of social connections—from the deep ties of family to more casual alliances with neighbors or even the barista at your favorite coffee shop. As a country kid this is what surprised me the most about city life: the connections with doormen, my barber, and the people who went to the gym at the same time made the city feel like a home.

What these different types of relationships share is that they are mutual—and provide a sense of belonging and support. These are the people you value and care for, who, in turn, value and care for you. It's important to realize that not every connection is meant to have the same depth and meaning. Your spouse, for example, should be on a different relationship plane than, say, the guy at work who shares your love of the local food scene. That might seem obvious, but what I often see people miss is that both of these relationships are beneficial to your mental health. They both provide different kinds of support—whether it's to help you take care of your family or to share tasty restaurant recommendations.

So, what's keeping us from making these varied connections in the modern world?

To start, distance. Our ancestors often stayed with their families, even once they paired up and started having children of their own. Outside the US, it's not uncommon to still see extended families sharing the same compounds or living within the same few blocks of one another, forming the backbone of a tight-knit community. Back in the day, it was the same in the US—and still is in some parts of the country, like rural Indiana, where I grew up. Fifty years ago, both in the city and countryside, you'd often see multiple generations cohabitating in the same domicile. And you'd regularly run into your extended family members around town or during monthly family get-togethers. These days, however, families have fewer children and our greater family networks are smaller. And, as I noted earlier, we are more likely to move away from our extended families when we reach adulthood, whether we are heading to college or seeking work. That means that you may not just run into your social contacts in the wild. You have to do more work to keep them up. This makes the modern world more of a challenge for connections, and by extension, our mental health.

I've been doing a lot of work on this myself after moving to Indiana, and now Wyoming. I tried joining a choral group and finding a pickup basketball game, which had always worked for me in the past. Neither ended up working out here in the West. Along with the barre class I discovered, I was thrilled when I began to bump into other dads I knew out hiking on the mountain trails or while snowboarding with our kids. All this is to say, we connect in different ways in different places. Consider the adaptations you may need to make to foster better connections; it's a great place to spend some time for your Mental Fitness. Be patient. Be consistent. Keep connecting.

Our institutions and neighborhoods are also changing. For example, just a few decades ago, you would probably find the house of worship your family subscribed to quite close to your home. These churches, mosques, meetinghouses, and synagogues didn't just provide weekly services—clergy members and volunteers knew each member of the congregation, would visit people who couldn't make it to the building for whatever reason. They would also arrange regular community events, from after-school programs to spaghetti nights, to bring people together. But, with congregation sizes dwindling, many of these community institutions have consolidated or closed down altogether. If you even still attend some kind of religious service, you are likely driving a good bit to get there—and you may not know most of the other people in attendance.

Now, there were certainly some downsides to having all these different kinds of close-knit community connections. No doubt there were plenty of people up in your business. But these kinds of community setups didn't just make it easier to socialize—they also made it easier to find support when you needed it. Neighbors would drop off casseroles when you were sick or in mourning. Family members could help watch your kids while you worked or went to school. There was usually someone around to hang out with if you wanted to socialize. Today, however, nearly half of Americans report that they don't know their neighbors. And most have few friends outside of their immediate families.

What else is interfering with creating a strong social network? You probably know what I'm going to say next: social media. Today the average social media user has virtual contact with hundreds of people every single day. What a big social network! Yet more than sixty percent of the population, across generational and geographic boundaries, report, like Ronnie, feeling lonely and isolated. We are the most interconnected generation in history. Yet, in a stroke of irony, we are the most starved for true connection. The downsides of social media have raised enough of an alarm when it comes to positively connecting with others that Surgeon General Murthy has suggested that we put a warning label on it.

Why might that be? Consider what we're really doing online. We look at the seemingly picture-perfect lives of others and hold our own up for comparison. We work hard to put up content that makes us look a certain way. We are constantly inundated with news (not to mention misinformation) that makes us feel anxious and sad. We spend an inordinate amount of time arguing with strangers when we could be talking to friends and neighbors as the algorithms favor controversy. Over time, it makes it more difficult for us to foster new connections. When I suggested to Ronnie, who is a huge Pittsburgh Steelers fan, that there was likely a group in town that met up to watch the games, he told me he already belonged to an online group that discusses the games.

"Are you making plans to hang out with anyone in that online group?" I asked him.

"Well, no," he said. "We just make jokes or talk about the coaches and ref calls online."

"Wouldn't it be more fun to watch the game with other people?"

"Of course!" he said. "But I wouldn't know anyone in one of those groups. I wouldn't even know who to talk to or what to say. And, online, I am watching the game with other people. I just don't necessarily know who they are."

Connecting has fundamentally changed with the dawn of social media. We interact with others in new ways as we scroll, like, comment, and start online arguments with political foes. Now, I am not here to tell you that social media is all bad. Every day, I interact with dozens of people on my own social media feeds. Most I will never meet—but many offer me encouraging feedback about my work and certainly give me a sense of greater community.

But we can't pretend that this new era of human connection is the same as what we found in real-world communities. And we seem to be struggling to adapt as quickly as we need to—and not recognizing the differences is incredibly risky, especially for adolescent brains.

A 2021 study of one million adolescents from over thirty-five countries, for example, found that adolescents are on a number of social networks—yet they report feeling socially isolated and lacking in social trust. This age group is more "connected" than ever, yet they aren't getting what they need from those digital relationships. But it's not just teenagers. Even adults who are avid social media users are experiencing disconnection—with a recent survey finding that seventy-three percent of heavy social media users considered themselves lonely, as compared to fifty-two percent of light users. We are digitally hyperconnected, yet feeling more and more disconnected. And it's why this particular tenet of Mental Fitness has the most potential to profoundly change your life. Real human connection is the tenet of Mental Fitness that can most powerfully and palpably affect you.

Even Ronnie, who came of age in a different time, can have trouble seeing the differences between virtual relationships and real ones. He's connected to his extended family on social media. He'll look at photos of his cousins' kids—or congratulate his brother-in-law on a work promotion. But when I asked about the last time he picked up the phone to have a real conversation with these people, he told me he couldn't remember.

"I guess it's easier to just like a photo than to call someone up out of the blue," he said. "I don't want to bother them."

There's that fear and anxiety again. But Ronnie would do far better to make that call or schedule a weekend visit. Because it's entirely likely that he's not the only one feeling socially isolated. His cousins, his brother-in-law, heck, even other Steelers fans at a local meet-up are likely going to benefit from face time as much as he is. (Let's face it—Ronnie is not alone. Many people struggled to jumpstart their social lives after the isolation of the COVID pandemic.)

All this is to say that the original, actual face time is important. Scientists are learning that face-to-face social interactions are much better for us than digital ones. While there is a lot we can do via computer screen, multiple studies have found that, when compared to digital communications, face-to-face social interactions are associated with increases in personal self-esteem and overall psychological well-being. Video calls are a great tool for my telemedicine practice but most people want to meet me in person at some point. There is something deeply human about being together IRL.

Making time for these kinds of real-world connections may seem harder these days because our attention spans are shorter—and well, they are often just more optional than before. We seem to have less time and less bandwidth for our relationships. But I'm here to tell you that it is important to make time, especially as we age. Because when we neglect our in-person, face-to-face relationships, our mental health suffers.

When I talk to my older patients in their sixties and seventies, they tell me over and over again how much their relationships matter to them. Ronnie, who isn't quite that age but is coming close, is recognizing how much his life is missing without those connections, too. That's why we need to start thinking about ways to nourish our social connections—and do so now. It's an exercise that will only strengthen your Mental Fitness.

CONNECTIONS FOR HEALTHY BRAINS

My excitement for psychiatry began with a serious enthusiasm for brain cells. I remain fascinated by the inner workings of neurons, synapses, and neurotransmitters. I remember learning in my first biology class that function is related to structure. That is, how something is built tells you a lot about what it does.

The human brain is an organ of connection. Every adaptation, every facet of your mental health is built to respond to interactions with your tribe. To socialize, to engage, and to converse. So, what happens to the brain when social paradigms shift more and more toward isolation?

I think about this a lot when I consider the benefits of human connection. Neurons, after all, are designed to connect. Brains have a big job to do—and they cannot do it without our brain cells firing and wiring together. That's why I see connection as a prime directive—we are better together—and why I ask all of my patients about their social connections to better assess their overall mental health. I'm creating a map of their personal web of connections. Who are the characters in this story and what is the quality of my patient's connection to them?

MAPPING OUT YOUR CONNECTIONS

As noted in the research, you want to have a diverse web of social connections: friends, family, acquaintances, and that guy you share smoothie recipes with at yoga class. To better understand your social connections, take some time to map out your people. Write the names of the people in your life who fall under the following categories:

Romantic Partner(s)/Spouse

Immediate Family

Extended Family

Friends

Neighbors

Acquaintances

Colleagues

Role Models

Mentors

Classmates

Spiritual Community Members

Volunteer Community Members

This list is not exhaustive. There may be other categories that make sense given where you are in life. Roommates, study partners, activity partners, club members, industry connections, or teammates. You determine the people who make up your social life—you can determine which categories best exemplify the people who make up your world. The key here is to take inventory so you can be more aware of where you spend most of your social capital—and where you might be able to expand your social circles to create more diverse connections.

Now, a confession: I had some concerns about my own mental health as I sat down to write this chapter. After years of living on the family farm with my parents, in the Indiana community where I grew up, I now sit over two thousand miles away in Wyoming. As the darkness of winter descended on me, I realized that this move meant that I'd lost quite a few of the connections that I've relied on over the decades. But, as I thought more about the people I'd left in Indiana, I realized I didn't really "lose" them. My family and friends, though now farther away, are still in my life. I just need to think more about how to nourish those relationships when I'm not living in proximity. I realized I needed to see the transition in my life and the meaning of creating our own home. And, as I was sorting through these feelings, I needed to take action to start creating a local support system of new friends and acquaintances. As you know, none of this happens overnight. Building connections takes time and effort.

A healthy brain is a connected brain. Structure equals function. By the same token, a healthy human is a connected human. And through winter sports, my local colleagues, and my kids' activities, my wife and I are finding ways to build our network here. In doing so, we are giving our brains what they need to thrive. I so clearly remember the first Friday night we were invited to a potluck by a group of new neighbors. I spent the evening chatting, laughing, and beaming. Feeling connected is sometimes wonderfully simple like this.

It's also a matter of survival. Several studies have now shown that human connection and attention are forms of medicine. One of the most well-known, a meta-analysis conducted in 2010 by researchers at Brigham Young University, looked at nearly 150 studies to assess the extent to which social relationships influence risk of mortality. The scientists found that having strong social relationships helps keep us alive longer—regardless of age, sex, or our health status.

Those social connections are also, literally, helping to keep our brains healthier. Having social support helps to increase brain-derived neurotrophic factor levels by about twenty-seven percent. While the researchers in this study were looking at social support and its influence on the development of dementia or stroke, we know that BDNF is directly correlated with the brain being in grow mode. Being around other people not only helps stave off mental decline, but also improves mood—and, as a consequence, mental health and well-being.

Other studies show that social support helps to reduce bodily inflammation. This is of benefit to the whole body, as excessive, dysregulated inflammation is linked to a wide variety of different health conditions. But we also know that brain inflammation is associated with depression and anxiety symptoms.

Social connections even play a role in promoting microbiome diversity. In a study out of the University of California, San Diego, researchers had 184 participants fill out self-reported measures of loneliness, social support, and social engagement. Even after controlling for age and body mass index, they found that people who reported higher levels of social support and engagement (and lower scores on the loneliness metrics), showed more diversity in the gut microbiome. This is yet another way our social networks can help us stay mentally fit.

There's something else worth mentioning here. Being with others just plain feels good. Whether you are spending quality time with your kids or just realized that the waitress at your favorite lunch spot remembers your name or your favorite dessert, these relationships remind you that you belong—and you matter.

The risks associated with a lack of in-person direct connection are neither ethereal nor simply abstract. In studies, people exhibiting habits of loneliness show markedly higher levels of depression and anxiety. They are at fifty percent higher risk of developing dementia. And don't forget that stat we mentioned earlier—they are more likely to experience a premature death, much like regular smokers.

It's time to take a long, hard look at your connections.

BUILDING STRONG CONNECTIONS IN THE MODERN WORLD

Studies and polls show that one in four Americans has exactly zero friends they feel capable of confiding in. That is a staggering statistic—and that number is only expected to grow. Fostering human connection, deepening the connections you have, and expanding the group of people you trust and confide in is one of the fundamental tenets of cultivating Mental Fitness. It's one of the ways I know in my clinical practice that my patients are getting better.

But, as you read this, I'm sure you are asking an important question: What is a good social connection, then? I'll tell you.

A good social connection is one that makes you feel cared for, valued, or appreciated. And, as I said before, they aren't all going to be ride-or-die type friendships. You want to have a diverse network of social connections—and you want to understand that these connections are meant to evolve over time. What you get from the connection, as well as what you put into maintaining it, will and must change depending on what's happening in your life.

For example, these days, I'm all about my kids. As they are reaching their teen years, I recognize that I have only a few years left where they'll want to hang out with me on the weekends. I'm consciously focused on this. Mind you, I'm not ignoring my spouse or friends to do so. But I am purposely saying no to certain things so I can ensure we have quality time to play, to cook, and just to talk. I'm giving the last piggyback rides of fatherhood. They already started to spend more time with their peers, signaling I should do the same. As I've noted, connections change. This can be a hard life lesson for some people. It's a bittersweet one for me.

My spouse and kids are my deepest connections these days. But I also put a high premium on relationships that might not, to the average person, seem like they should matter so much. One of my mentors at medical school—someone whom I once spoke to for hours each week—has now become someone I speak to only a few times a year. But when we do see each other at medical meetings, or we just call on the phone, we pick up where we left off. I'm certain you have similar people in your life. I don't need that kind of mentor as much. But our connection is still one that makes me feel seen, appreciated, and reassured, even all these years later.

So perhaps it's not surprising that social psychology studies suggest that people who report strong feelings of well-being have a diverse portfolio of social connections. Researchers at Harvard

Business School were originally trying to determine the *best* kind of relationship to have to help bolster your mental and emotional health. After conducting a survey about different kinds of relationships, they discovered something surprising. The people who reported feeling the best about themselves were those who had a unique mix of relationships. The higher number of different relationship categories they interacted with day to day, the happier they reported themselves to be. Weaker ties seem to be just as important to our mental health as the strong ones.

You want to have a great relationship with your significant other, your children, and your parents, of course. But you also gain value from having daily conversations with friends, acquaintances, coworkers, and even seemingly random people. The guy you always see on the Q train. The barista at your favorite coffee shop. The other parents at your kid's soccer games. The supermarket checkout person. Making time and space for those connections helps cultivate Mental Fitness, too. And by engaging in those interactions, you may find, without too much overt work on your part, that what were once more fleeting connections grow deeper.

The world is changing. Today, more and more people are working remotely. Our social structures, many of which support community interactions, are changing. The very constructs that help us be more social are being reimagined and reconfigured as part of this new, modern, and digital lifestyle. Much of that opens up new avenues for human interaction. But it also means that the old ways of connecting may not work as they used to. That we may have to push a little harder, move out of our comfort zones, and find ways to connect that may feel a little unfamiliar.

I could relate. During the pandemic, my clinical work became one hundred percent telemedicine overnight. Connection is essential to effective work as a therapist and people would frequently ask me if teletherapy was "as good" as in-person therapy. It turns out it was different and in some cases much better. Another part that now seems obvious. Over time, my skills improved and my ideas about telemedicine evolved. I saw some clinical scenarios that I never would have encountered before like a new father who regularly brought his son to his weekly sessions. With telemedicine, I am able to meet all the pets and often a few family members. Sometimes patients use their screens to share their work or family photos. Contrary to my initial concerns, the depth and richness of our connection seemed to increase in new and exciting ways.

I told as much to Ronnie. We started working by talking about ways to expand his social network. He opted to reach out to some of his old coworkers to see if they could catch up—and try that Steelers meet-up group. It may seem silly, but building connections is really about the small stuff. Starting a conversation, remembering past interactions, and really listening to what people say to you. It's these small acts that help to build big connections.

We also talked about his dating life. Ronnie had given up on online dating sites because he wasn't finding someone with whom he wanted to make a long-term commitment. But I asked him if he could deemphasize the goal of finding a spouse—and instead think about dating as just meeting new people. Dating doesn't always have to be about finding your perfect life partner. But just the act of going out with new people can help you foster important skills that will aid you once you do meet that special someone—active listening, communication, and compromise.

"I mean, eventually, I'd like to have a partner again," he said. "But I suppose it could be fun to have someone to go out to do stuff with."

So, time for some Mental Fitness homework. Take a good look at your own social network. Not your Instagram followers—or that political pundit whom you like to argue with on that divisive social media platform. Think about the people you talk to day to day. Who are you connecting with? How diverse is that network? Pick up a pen and write it down. As I mentioned earlier, I like to think about this as a map or a web of connection and writing it down can be helpful, too.

If you are feeling lonely or isolated, you can work with what you have. Send a note, text, or DM to your best friend from college. (A high school friend recently sent our kids a postcard from a trip to Antarctica and it really touched my heart.) Ask a friend to join you for a walk or exercise class. Join a book club. Finally sign up for art or guitar lessons. ("Stairway to Heaven"!) Explore a spiritual community or church, if that's your thing. Or you can take Dr. Murthy's 5 for 5 Connection Challenge. The US Surgeon General literally made a Connect Deck, offering suggestions for ways you can meaningfully connect with others over a five-day period.

Anyone can expand their community and diversify their social portfolio. And while many experts emphasize the importance of conversation to strengthening social connections, I think it is even more important to *listen*. Pay attention to what they say and what matters to them. Be there for them when you can. The idea is to listen to other people actively. Often this provides just as much benefit to you, the person doing the listening. It puts our own problems in perspective and shows us our own ability to be helpful to others. It's the big secret I have learned from twenty years of professional listening. Most often people need an ear, not an expert.

It's not always easy, but when you try to connect with others with consistency, awareness, and reciprocity, you will find that you reap what you sow. It certainly happened with Ronnie. Within a few months, he had met a couple of guys who were also divorced empty-nesters. They started getting together regularly to grab dinner, watch sports, or just hang out. His network expanded more when one of those guys invited him to join a monthly poker game.

"It's been a lot of fun," he said. "I'm meeting new people, and to be honest, I'm not sure what I was so anxious about before."

Ronnie said one of the best things about these friends is that they also check up on one another. He said that recently, when his son was home from college, he skipped the poker game. He received a couple of texts asking if all was well.

"It's nice to know that you're missed. One guy, when he heard that my son would be leaving at the end of the week, asked if I wanted to grab dinner that night. He said he remembered how hard it was when he dropped his kids back at school. That meant a lot," he said. "Now, if I haven't heard from someone for a while, I'll send a quick text message or maybe a funny meme just to let them know I'm here if they need me. I'll also make sure to ask about grabbing some food or hanging out if I think they might be having a hard time."

Connection, in regards to Mental Fitness, is necessary, not discretionary—even for those of us who may identify as introverts. Your brain is constantly reaching out for new connections, and by prioritizing the need for socializing, you can create better context for mental health and better overall quality of life.

But as you look to expand your social connections, remember: There's no one-size-fits-all relationship. Our different connections in life serve us in different ways. Some people need us to show up in different ways than others. We need the various connections in our lives for different reasons. And when you start to recognize the value of a rich, colorful tapestry of social connections to bolster your Mental Fitness, you'll see the power the people around you have in healing the modern brain.

UNDERSTANDING THE DIFFERENCE BETWEEN BEING ALONE AND BEING LONELY

Part of developing a diverse portfolio of social connections is also building a relationship with yourself. While there has been a wealth of studies talking about the negative consequences of social isolation, there is value in spending time alone. Part of Mental Fitness is learning to enjoy your own company.

First, let's define the terms "loneliness" and "being alone." While there is some overlap, they are different. Loneliness is a feeling of emptiness—and it can occur even when you have company. In fact, some people may feel lonely even when they are in a relationship—or even in a crowd. Loneliness is a distinct state of mind, a feeling of disconnection that makes you feel unseen, unheard, and unappreciated.

Being alone, of course, is a bit different. You aren't interacting with others in the moment. For some people, alone time is incredibly beneficial. It gives us the opportunity to rest, relax, and focus on ourselves. But if your social network is so small that you can't find people to interact with when you are actively trying to, it can become a problem. It can grow into social isolation and loneliness. That's when it becomes an issue.

Over the years, I've worked with many patients who are lonely because they have never treated their social anxiety disorder with anything other than alcohol or drugs. Many of my patients who have experienced trauma also face difficulties being relaxed and comfortable around others. But addressing loneliness really is about scheduling and framework. If you are feeling lonely, you can attend a sporting event or go check out some live music. Even going out to grab some groceries is inherently social—and provides the opportunity to interact with others and enjoy the connections we share with each other.

If you are feeling lonely, it's important not to let it grow into true social isolation. In 2019, Swiss researchers discovered that social isolation was associated with an *elevenfold* increase in the risk of moderate to severe depression. Social isolation also makes it more likely that you will ignore other tenets of Mental Fitness—studies have found that people who are socially isolated are more likely to have a poor diet and live more sedentary lives. These things, as we know, also increase the risk of mental illness.

As a clinician, and as someone who has struggled with

mood issues in the past, I know how much harder it is to address mental health concerns when you are isolated. It's a self-perpetuating cycle, which only exacerbates depressive symptoms. That's why it is so important to engage with others so you can build stronger connections with the individuals and institutions that can provide you support. I would also add that our brains benefit when we reach out to serve others. Whether it is just holding open a door for a stranger, checking in on an old friend, or volunteering at the local soup kitchen, helping others is a remarkably powerful way to connect. When we are hurting, we hope that people help us. But there's a great change in mindset when we help others. We see the simple human power to connect. We create the very thing that we want in our own lives—and this, friends, is profoundly healing.

CHAPTER 8

Engagement

Elise lived alone in a small, suburban cookie-cutter apartment not far from her job. When she signed the lease in the sprawling residential complex three years earlier, she saw the move as a symbol of newfound independence. She was making enough to live on her own terms. No roommates, no compromise. It was a big deal to her.

Now, each morning, she made a twenty-minute commute to the large technology company where she had a supervisory role at a busy call center. It was a good job with great benefits. But it wasn't where she thought she'd be when she graduated from college more than a decade before.

"I feel like I have the same conversations over and over again," she said. "Both with the customers who call us—and the people who work for me. It gets really old, really quickly."

The walls, she told me, are painted the barely noticeable beige that one associates with dentists' offices and department store dressing rooms. And since corporate policy dictated that employees can only have one piece of "flair" to decorate cubicles, Elise made do with a photo of her and her family taken on their last vacation to the beach. It didn't do much to break up the monotony of her days.

"I shouldn't complain," she said. "Everyone said I wouldn't even find a job if I majored in English—and this is a really good gig. They pay me well. The benefits are amazing. There is a clear path to promotion. It's just not the most exciting work. But, you know, in this economy, I don't know if it's even realistic to expect to have exciting work. You want a reliable paycheck. And I have a reliable paycheck."

But when I asked Elise to tell me about what she does for fun—how she uses that reliable paycheck to do the things that bring her joy—she expressed the same sense of futility.

"When I get home from work, I'm usually pretty beat," she said. "I'll make myself something to eat, watch something on Netflix, and then scroll Instagram for a while. Nothing too crazy."

"What about on the weekends?" I ask. "What do you do then?"

"Oh, I don't know," she said. "Every once in a while, I'll hang out with friends. But everyone's so busy. And lots of my friends are at these different life stages now. Some are married. Some have kids. It's harder to want to reach out."

"Have you seen your family lately?"

"We talk once a week or so." She shrugged. "But, when we do talk, my mom is always asking me what I'm doing. I don't really feel like I have anything to tell her. I'm sure she doesn't want to hear about how boring work is again."

"What about engaging in other activities?" I asked. "You said you were an English major. Have you read any good books lately? Maybe thought about joining a book club?"

"I can't remember the last book I read," she said. "I think maybe I used up my allotment of reading hours back in college."

I couldn't help but notice that Elise expressed the same sense of futility about every aspect of her life. She was disengaged—and, if she were forty years older and expressed these same feelings to a gerontologist, they would be concerned enough that they'd recommend that she start making some pretty significant lifestyle changes.

Why might that be? The latest scientific studies now show that there is a significant link between a lack of cognitive engagement and dementia. While we often talk about dementia as a specific disease, something akin to Alzheimer's disease, it's really more of a category of symptoms that characterize an impaired ability to remember, make decisions, or problem-solve as you get older. This goes beyond the so-called senior moments that you might have as you age, where you misplace your reading glasses or take an extra few seconds to remember a word or recall an acquaintance's name. These are significant cognitive impairments that interfere with day-to-day functioning and independent living. As such, it's something you want to avoid—or at least delay—if at all possible. And keeping your brain engaged through meaningful activities throughout your life is one way to do that. Because, as it turns out, if you don't use it—meaning, your brain—you can, in fact, lose it.

Not only is there that link between a lack of cognitive engagement and dementia, but a host of new neuroscientific studies also demonstrate a strong association between depression and dementia. Many experts now suggest that depression is both a risk factor and potentially a prodrome for, or early symptom of, dementia. Interestingly enough, both depression and dementia share an interesting feature: inflammation.

We've already discussed how inflammation is a mental health killer. Chronic inflammation can lead to inadvertent damage to healthy cells and tissues in the brain. This can lead to a lot of downstream problems. Case in point: psychopathological studies suggest that the same inflammatory brain pathologies that lead to depression and mild cognitive impairment, over time, have the power to ultimately progress to dementia.

This is why, even though Elise was decades away from an AARP membership, I was equally as concerned about her lack of cognitive engagement. It wasn't just that she was disconnected from other people. We already talked about why that's a problem—and why her lack of social connections was likely contributing to declining mental health. But Elise was also not engaging her mind, either at work or at home. And that, too, had the power to negatively influence her Mental Fitness.

That's right. Cultivating Mental Fitness literally requires finding ways to exercise your mind. Staying sharp is yet another way you can help heal the modern brain.

A BRAIN MADE FOR COGNITIVE ENGAGEMENT

To understand the importance of cognitive engagement we must once again rewind back about twelve thousand years. Yes, let's revisit our old friends, the hunter-gatherers. We've already talked quite a bit about how their needs have helped to shape our brains—and shaped them in ways that have been evolutionarily preserved even today.

As our ancestors explored the forests and savannas, their very survival required them to develop strong problem-solving skills. The ability to think on your feet was a serious benefit. Let's start with finding enough food to satisfy you and your in-group. You'd need to maintain a cursory knowledge of satiating plants—as well as the best places to find them. Bonus points if they were safe to eat and tasty to the palate. Once hunting was added to the repertoire, knowing the habits of animals you were trying to snare would also be of great use in trying to feed the family. But you couldn't rest on your laurels. Seasons change, migration patterns change, times change. You had to up your hunting-and-gathering game in order to stay fed. And so you had to stay cognitively sharp, increasing your knowledge and your know-how to make sure everyone was obtaining enough to eat.

Cognitive engagement offers similar benefits when it comes to avoiding predators in the wild. Survival would require collecting and storing important information about the world around you. Having a sharp memory about the stalking habits of lions, tigers, and other sharp-toothed baddies will help keep you safe. Understanding not only what venomous snakes and spiders look like, but where they make their homes, will make it easier to give them a wide berth. Then there's using your noggin to take things a step further by raising sleeping areas off the ground, keeping fires burning throughout the night, and painting eyes on landmarks so predators think they are being watched, too.

And you can't forget about engaging the brain to find shelter. Sure, initially, you might have been lucky enough to find a nice cave or a well-placed formation of trees to protect you from the elements. But, by learning how to weave those long savanna grasses into water-resistant mats and using wood and stones to dig a pit house, you could provide yourself and your family a much more substantial place to rest your head.

I could go on, but the point is that our brains learned, remembered, and continued to evolve over time. They are designed to do just that. The very neuroplasticity, or "grow mode" that we talk about as being so good for mental health, is what underlies learning. The brain's innate ability to adapt and change, to form new synaptic connections, is what allows us to learn what we need to so we can navigate the world around us. When we find ourselves in a position where we are no longer learning, our brains start to stagnate. That's where mental health problems, as well as neurodegeneration, begin.

I'm not saying that you need to give up your creature comforts and start living off-grid to maximize your brain health. But it's important to remember that our brains like a good challenge. Whether that involves learning something new, trying to solve a good jigsaw puzzle, or diving into the latest bestselling book, the brain thrives when we can find ways to keep it engaged.

WHAT'S STOPPING COGNITIVE ENGAGEMENT IN THE MODERN WORLD

While it would be all too easy to point the finger at technology as the culprit for a decrease in cognitive engagement—and certainly, with international academic test scores dropping in correlation with greater adoption of smartphones, many are making such an argument—it's not quite so simple. There are plenty of studies that show that younger people in particular who spend more time on devices tend to do worse in school and have more problems overall with their mental health. Yet I think it's important to take a step back. Smartphones are a tool. And like any other tool, it's what we do with them that matters.

Today, we all tend to stay within arm's reach of our smartphones. We use these magic devices to communicate, to navigate, to research, to purchase, to take photos and video, to figure out how to thaw a turkey, to read books, to watch our favorite shows, to unlock our cars, to play games, to monitor our heart rates, to light our way, to figure out where our kids are, and so much more. They are a veritable Swiss Army knife of applications. And they make things incredible easy and convenient.

On one hand, that's great. You have a one-stop shop in a small three-by-five device. You can offload a lot of effort—and anyone who has DoorDashed a hot meal after a hard day at the office understands the appeal. On the other hand, letting your phone handle all the hard stuff doesn't always serve us when it comes to engaging our brains. Our brains learn by doing—and when we try new things, explore, problem-solve, and think things through, our neurons grow and connect. When we are relying on our devices to make those connections for us, our brains, over time, lose out.

Elise, for example, foisted a lot of heavy lifting onto her devices. She did the majority of her shopping online, with a preset grocery list that instantly uploaded to a delivery service each Saturday. She had an app that automatically sent flowers to her mother and sister on their birthdays. She had an at-home smart assistant device that managed everything from her thermostat to her television. She fully admitted that she relied on technology to think and do less.

"Isn't that the whole point of all these apps and devices?" she said. "To free your bandwidth for other stuff?"

That's exactly the point I'm trying to make. No one says you should have to spend your precious free time tracking down the phone number for a flower shop or doing grocery shopping if you don't want to. But if you are "freeing up your bandwidth" with technology, the idea is that you should be filling it with something else that is going to give your brain a bit of a workout. Far too often, thanks to technology, our worlds are becoming smaller. That means there's less room for our brains to stretch. That needs to change.

MAKING TIME FOR A MENTAL WORKOUT

The other week, my wife, Lucy, and I went to a barre class in town. This form of physical exercise, which takes foundational ballet movements and adds them to a funky beat, is designed to strengthen the legs and core. As an avid horseback rider, I had been looking for ways to make exactly those improvements—and the online horseback riding community had waxed poetic about the power of barre for both balance and strength. About twenty minutes into the class, I realized I was very much out of my element. Not only was I one of only two men in a class full of very coordinated women, but I had never moved my body in quite this way before. Here I was, a somewhat lanky, six-foot, one-inch man, holding the barre with a death grip. I had been told to simply rest my fingertips on it for balance—but, in order not to fall on my face, I was gripping it so hard there was a distinct possibility I might pull it out of the wall. When the instructor told us to start maneuvering our bodies toward the floor on a four count, while shaking our hips from side to side, I might have dissociated for a moment. But somehow, someway, I got through the whole class.

Later, as I thought more about the experience, I realized something. I wasn't just working my glutes (although I was, indeed, working my glutes—and felt it for days afterward). I was also working my brain. Trying new moves, in a new environment, gave my mental health a real boost. Exercising your brain, whether it be in this kind of scenario or a completely different one, can do the same for you.

I'm not the only one to realize this. While there aren't a lot of studies that look at the direct effects of engagement on mental health, psychiatrists and mental health professionals are noting that people who partake in various hobbies, as well as engage in lifelong learning activities, receive a lot of brain benefits. This has led the United Kingdom's National Health Service to now recommend that people who are trying to improve their mood and overall well-being learn new skills, whether it be learning to cook or working on a do-it-yourself project, to boost their self-confidence and self-esteem, as well as connect with other people.

The studies that are in the literature have pretty promising results—so much so that some in the medical community are suggesting that it's time we start prescribing cognitive engagement to our patients (or at least heartily recommending it). A study in a Japanese community of older adults found that people who did not have hobbies were not only more likely to score higher on measures of depression but also laughed a lot less frequently than people who put time into activities like sewing, model-making, or music. In 2019, researchers at University College London did an analysis of nearly 9,000 individuals showing that, controlling for all other variables, taking up a hobby was associated with a decrease in depressive symptoms for those who were experiencing them, as well as thirty percent lower odds of ever experiencing depression. When they broke down the different activities to look at the contributions of demographics, health-related variables, reading habits, social engagement, and physical activity factors, they accounted for only about one-quarter of the effect. Seventy-seven percent of the association could be attributed to the enjoyment and cognitive engagement of the hobby itself.

One of the best things about this study is that there doesn't seem to be anything special about any one activity over another. You can engage in the hobby that you enjoy the most. Are you into crocheting or knitting? Go for it. Do you like to paint or sculpt? Awesome. Maybe you are a fan of flower arranging or photography. If you are actively engaged in the activity and you enjoy it, it's going to benefit you. So go find your jam.

It's worthwhile to mention that there is also a lot of benefit in being a lifelong learner. This is another aspect of cognitive engagement. It's one that we may not talk about enough—and, honestly, when you are really into a particular activity, we may not have to. If you enjoy what you are doing enough, you likely are on the lookout for new ways to grow and learn. You want to find the next challenge to keep things fresh.

That helps the brain stay in grow mode, too. And studies in the social psychological realm show that lifelong learners, that is, people who are self-motivated to continue voluntarily pursuing skills and knowledge no matter their stage in life, either in a formal or informal setting, show a range of psychosocial benefits. A field-work study of lifelong learners demonstrated they reported greater well-being, with enhanced protection and recovery from stress and mental health difficulties. They had higher self-esteem and self-efficacy, or belief in their own abilities. They also had a stronger sense of purpose and hope. These are all things that help to sustain Mental Fitness over the long term.

As you think about how you can add a mental workout into your own life, it's important to remember that, like physical exercise, there's no one-size-fits-all approach. If you were to search the internet, you'd likely find a listicle about brain exercises that would include options like sudoku and some kind of online jigsaw puzzle. But there's more to cognitive engagement than online games. What you are looking for is something that will challenge you—and give your brain an opportunity to learn and grow. For me, that was taking up regular barre classes, even if I might be the awkward duckling in a mirrored room full of graceful swans. For others, that might be the challenge of reading all the books on the Great American Novels list. Some might sign up for a woodworking or beekeeping class. Still others might decide it's finally time to learn a new language or to join the local choir. Don't forget the possibilities of a good dance class—as you might remember, Australian researchers found it was one of the best forms of exercise. They hypothesized that one reason it was so beneficial was the fact that it not only engaged the muscles, but also engaged the brain.

But you can decide to do whatever you want. The only requirement is that it engages you, it pushes you out of your comfort zone a little, and you enjoy it. This is what will help keep your brain circuits active, drive down inflammation, and support Mental Fitness over the long term.

CREATING A HOBBY ALGORITHM

Growing up, you probably had a number of hobbies. As we grow older, we often put those leisure activities aside for the "important" things: work and family. It's not always so easy to pick them back up again. If you are trying to decide how to bring more engagement into your life, I suggest creating a hobby algorithm. By asking yourself a few key questions, you can start to consider different options to try.

1. What kinds of activities did you enjoy as a kid?

2. Do you enjoy socializing in big groups? Or do you prefer smaller settings?

3. What kind of things are your friends doing? Where might you join them?

4. What kind of activities most relax you?

5. What kind of activities most invigorate you?

6. What activity have you always wanted to try? Why haven't you?

7. Who in your life could you tap as a hobby buddy?

8. What are some hobby options that you would like to try? Which include engagement, physical activity, and social aspects?

UPPING YOUR COGNITIVE RESERVE

Cognitive engagement also has the benefit of building up what's called cognitive reserve. It's not one thing per se, but the culmination of a lifetime of experiences that come together to help improve overall cognitive performance, as well as provide an extra bit of cognitive resilience as you grow older. Higher education helps to build up cognitive reserve. So does being bilingual. Playing a musical instrument also gives you a little extra cognitive reserve. There are a lot of different ways to gain this little extra cognitive oomph—and it's something you definitely want. Multiple studies have shown that cognitive reserve reduces your risk of mild cognitive impairment and dementia later in life—but it can also help mitigate the challenges we face from stress and other mental health issues earlier in life. That's why cognitive engagement is a core tenet of Mental Fitness, too.

Of course, building Mental Fitness doesn't require you to start doing sudoku every day—unless that's your jam. I've seen patients who manage to expand their engagement through tango dancing, surfing, improv classes, traveling cross-country, writing a novel, and much, much more. While it might be easy to say the benefits of some of these activities may be due to the physical or social aspects—and certainly, like my barre class experience, they likely play a role—the mental challenges involved with expanding your horizons are also a boon to mental health. When you help your brain forge new connections, you help your brain thrive.

Elise, it was immediately clear to me, was missing cognitive engagement. While finding another job that might provide more of a mental challenge might not be in the cards for her, developing social activities that could give her a mental boost became a priority. We talked about things she could do that would not only get her out of the house but also let her exercise her brain. When she mentioned that a friend invited her to a local poetry slam event, I asked her to tell me more. It was the first time in a while that she had sounded remotely interested in a social outing.

"It's a weekly thing at this coffee shop. They have three chosen poets who read their work," she said. "But then anyone can go up and read something if they want to."

"Didn't you do a lot of poetry in college as part of your major?" I asked.

"Well, yeah," she said. "But I haven't written anything in ages."

"What's stopping you from writing something now? Or reading something that you wrote when you were back in school?"

She paused for a moment. I could see that she was intrigued by the idea of participating, but also a little scared of jumping into the fray.

"I wouldn't even know where to begin with that," she replied with some hesitation.

"Maybe, this week, you go and listen," I said. "Then go back and read something later."

It took Elise about six weeks—after going to the first poetry slam, she was inspired to write something new—but she did go up onstage and read her poem.

"I thought I was going to throw up," she said. "But once I got the words out, the response was so amazing."

Within a few months, she was regularly writing again, filling notebooks with new poems whenever the muse struck. Equally important, Elise, who had been an avid reader for most of her life, was also tearing through books on the regular. Our sessions changed dramatically. No longer were they full of how boring and staid her life was—instead she was telling me about the new book she was reading, or the poem she was working on. She was also making plans to use her good salary—and solid vacation benefit—to head to a writers' retreat in the fall. Her brain was engaged, and it was paying off in dividends.

There's no one way to boost your cognitive reserve. The types of activities that will engage your brain and fire up your neurons will vary from person to person. The key is to find new challenges that interest you and promote creativity and cognitive flexibility. While some may say to pick up a musical instrument or to start learning a new language (both are tried and true for brain boosting), it's not always so clear-cut. I recommend looking for activities that offer you a combination of enjoyment, social aspects, and a bit of a mental challenge. For Elise, that was poetry. For you, that may be something else.

For example, another patient of mine, Adam, found his cognitive engagement in an auto mechanics class. Adam found himself in a bit of a funk after his father died. His dad had bequeathed him a classic 1968 Ford Mustang Shelby. Unfortunately, the car was in quite a state of disrepair. During one of our sessions, Adam recounted how he and his father had always talked about how they would fix it up one day.

"We always said we'd do it," he said. "But we never did."

"Is there any reason why you couldn't do it now?" I asked him.

"I don't know anything about cars," Adam said. "I doubt I could even identify a carburetor under duress."

"You could always learn."

"I've never been very good at that kind of typical guy stuff," he said. "I probably wouldn't be any good at it."

"Actually, I think you'd be quite good at it," I said. "It just takes a little time and focus."

About a year later, Adam decided to give auto mechanics a try. He signed up for a "powder puff" mechanics class at a local community college. It wasn't a class that would help him restore a classic car—but it could teach him the basics. And his instructors were immediately impressed to learn what a gem he had hiding in his garage.

What started as a whim for Adam became a treasured hobby. It was a way for him to feel close to his dad—and a way for him to meet new people. Over time, he moved from the basics to more sophisticated mechanics. Eventually he fixed up the Mustang. It became a point of pride for him. He felt like he kept an unspoken promise to his father—and, I believe, it helped him boost his Mental Fitness during what were some very trying years after his father's passing.

Cognitive engagement is not negotiable. It is imperative that you stay sharp—at any age. And as you look for ways to increase your own cognitive engagement, the first step is really to think about what you like to do. Because there are so many different ways to stimulate the brain. There's no one right way to do it.

You can engage with yourself. This could be reading, writing, jigsaw puzzles, learning a new language, practicing a musical instrument, working on challenging math problems, or woodworking.

You can engage with institutions. You can take a class, attend lectures at universities or museums, go to performances or concerts, make music with others, travel in a group, go to a comedy club, or volunteer with your favorite organizations.

You can engage with others. You can meet up with friends for conversations, join a debate or book club, take a religious study or discussion class, or find a way to learn about other perspectives.

This list is far from exhaustive—and certainly, you'll find overlaps with the other tenets of Mental Fitness. The trick is to just keep challenging yourself. If you like to hike, don't stick to the same old trails. Seek out some new routes to try. Talk to fellow hikers about their favorites. Join a local hiking group to make the activity more social. If you are a puzzle hound, head to the library to find more challenging options. See if they know of a puzzle meet-up in the area. Try the more challenging dance class. Plan that trip to Portugal. Speak to your new French neighbor *en français*.

Read. Write. Learn. Laugh. Explore. Embrace. Dance. Challenge yourself. Let your brain expand and grow—building your Mental Fitness in the process. Your mental health will thank you.

CHAPTER 9

Grounding

When I first learned I had been offered a residency spot in New York City, I was elated. I was very happy to have been accepted into the Adult Psychiatry program at Columbia University. I loved the idea of moving to the big, bad city. This Indiana farm boy intended to get out of the country—and fully partake in the city that never sleeps.

But fast-forward a few years and the daily commute between my family's small apartment in the West Village, up to the New York State Psychiatric Institute, and then to my private practice was taking its toll. With the addition of a wife and baby daughter, I realized I was living a "box to box" existence—going from one inside space to another, with little exposure to green space or sunlight. All those fluorescent lights and recycled air were getting to me. And I desperately missed being able to just step outside and lose myself in nature.

After spending a summer month back in Indiana on the farm with my family, I realized I wanted something different for our daughter. She was still only a toddler—but, as we packed to return to New York, I felt like I was robbing her of something essential. Growing up on a farm had provided me with a strong work ethic, a sense of self-efficacy, and a lot of fun adventures. I realized I wanted Greta to have the same freedoms I had as a kid and the same connection to nature. I could imagine her climbing trees, planting her own small garden plot, and catching tadpoles on the property's pond. We started making plans to return to Indiana the next summer. And the one after that.

We wouldn't make the decision to permanently return to the farm until our second child, Forrest, started to toddle. (He also started to struggle with asthma and the loud noises of the city.) While the idea of leaving New York wasn't an easy one, after spending those weeks in the country, it felt like the right thing to do for our kids. A way to move them out of a box-to-box indoor existence—and nurture their growing bodies and brains. I didn't know it at the time, but a whole host of scientific studies would soon be published that supported my intuitions.

As you can imagine, it wasn't just our kids who would benefit. Finding ways to bring more green nature into your life—to ground yourself by spending time in natural places and spaces—is a great way to help cultivate Mental Fitness and heal the modern brain.

THE MODERN URBAN LIFE

Today, more than half the world's population lives in or near a city. The United Nations expects that by 2050 that number will more than double—estimating that seven in ten people will reside in an urban area. Projections for the United States suggest close to ninety percent of people will eventually call the city, or the nearby suburbs, home. It makes sense. These are the places where you can find work, medical infrastructure, transportation access, and culture—just to name a few of the benefits that come with city living. Unfortunately, modern urban environments can also take a toll on both our physical and mental health.

Let's start with the noise. Cities are notoriously loud—and people who live there are regularly exposed to noise at eighty-five decibels or higher, thanks to traffic, industrial activity, and transportation hubs. That's the sound equivalent of running a blender or power lawn mower in the same room. Not only does this level of noise have the power to lead to significant hearing loss over time—experts recommend that sound levels stay under seventy decibels normally, and, if they go over eighty-five, they shouldn't do so for more than an hour—but it also increases the risk of a variety of health issues that have nothing to do with your ears.

People who live in noisy environments regularly have problems, including disturbed sleep and high blood pressure. And yes, they are at a higher risk of developing problems with their mental health, like clinical anxiety and depression. So, no, you weren't overreacting when you thought that loud construction noise (or your kid's deafening video game soundtrack) was sending you over the edge. All the extra noise can really take a toll on both our physical and mental well-being. Indeed, the World Health Organization is actively working with city governments all over the globe to come up with policies that will help make urban areas easier on the ears. In the meantime, I often recommend that my patients evaluate and decrease the noise stimulation in their lives whenever and wherever possible, by using noise-canceling headphones during their subway commute or just turning off the television during mealtimes.

Noise isn't the only environmental factor in cities that can affect your physiological systems. Consider all the artificial light you are exposed to in urban areas. Bright lights are the norm in many parts of the city—New York's Times Square, for example, is so bright that astronauts have literally been able to photograph the extra wattage all the way from outer space. While all those lights might be pretty, like noise they can wreak havoc on your nervous system. A recent study of more than 85,000 people demonstrated that greater nighttime light exposure was correlated with a significantly increased risk for depression, anxiety, and a whole host of other mental health disorders.

As we already discussed, our circadian rhythm, our internal body clock that governs waking and rest, is linked to the dark. Even a few hundred years ago, human beings didn't live with artificial lights. Once the sun went down, we went to sleep. While you could argue that the addition of electric lights has made us much more productive as a society, it has come at a cost. That extra light can knock your circadian rhythms out of whack—and reduce your body's natural melatonin production. Exposure to room lights versus dim light has been shown to decrease melatonin production by half! Room lights also decrease the onset and duration of melatonin's effect.

With this onslaught of noise and artificial light, the brain can have a hard time powering down when it's time to rest. Your attention systems remain on high alert to help ensure all those stimuli aren't a potential threat—and, as a result, your sleep quality suffers. Over time, even if you think, as many urban dwellers do, that you are impervious to the city sounds and sights, your brain isn't getting what it needs to work its best. It is harder to support routine rest and replenishment. Neurotrophic factor production, better known as "brain fertilizer," goes down. Inflammation goes up. The microbiome loses diversity. And if you don't find a way to address these environmental factors, your mental health can and will suffer.

These factors also can affect those living in suburbia. Here, too, you may be experiencing heightened noise and extra artificial light. You might just be rocking out to the sounds of a leaf blower instead of a jackhammer. Outside of the noise and light, it's likely that those in suburbia are also stuck in a box-to-box living situation— moving from your house, to your car, to your workplace, and then back again. Lather, rinse, repeat, day after day after day.

To heal the modern brain, we need to become a little antiquated. We need to start taking advantage of the places that provide us with space, quiet, and natural light. Our brains benefit when we do as our ancestors did—and regularly go back into nature.

DESIGNED FOR GREEN

Believe it or not, even if you are a fan of city living, your brain was designed to thrive in green spaces. From an evolutionary perspective, it makes sense. Go back a few thousand years, and human beings needed to be in tune with the great outdoors in order to survive. We needed to be able to discern predators and prey in the long, tall grasses and dense forests we traversed. Our ability to navigate outdoors helped us find food and shelter, not to mention avoid any potential dangers hidden in the weeds. Those basic needs—food, shelter, safety—shaped our brains in ways that still hold sway even today.

Take our vision. The human retina, directly wired to the brain, is calibrated to see green. That visible spectrum of color, those specific wavelengths between the blues and reds, is at the center of our visual range. As a result, it's where our perception is best. We require fewer cognitive resources to detect movement or see something hiding in greens. It makes sense: this kind of perception would be vital to human survival. It would help us find food, as well as stay away from venomous snakes or other predators.

Our vision isn't the only way humans have evolved in order to promote survival on this planet. Over the past few million years, we've developed a symbiotic relationship with plants. We *need* each other to stay alive. Humans breathe in the oxygen and exhale carbon dioxide. Plants do the very opposite. The by-product of photosynthesis, the basic biological process that helps plants grow, is an essential element for our own growth and survival. And, of course, having a constant supply of oxygen plays a key role in keeping your brain healthy and in grow mode.

It's also worth mentioning that plants provide us with more than just oxygen. Trees, for example, release unique compounds called phytoncides. These antimicrobial organic compounds help plants fight disease. They do the same for us. When we breathe these fascinating compounds in with our oxygen, they lead to changes in our immune systems. Japanese researchers have shown that when humans spend time in the forest and are exposed to these chemicals, it improves immune function by increasing the number of special immune fighting cells, called natural killer cells. These are special white blood cells that act as deadly assassins against viruses and tumors, helping to keep us fit and healthy. Of course, over time this helps to reduce inflammation in the body—and our brains.

THIS IS YOUR BRAIN ON NATURE

Ruth, a sixtysomething Manhattanite, first came to see me a few years after she lost her husband, Rob, to aggressive lung cancer. When she and Rob first started courting, they'd often borrow a car, grab a gourmet picnic, and spend the day on the beach in Montauk or hiking up Bear Mountain. Later in life, careers and kids got in the way of regular sojourns outside the city. After Rob's death, Ruth found herself even more isolated, alone with her grief in a small, rent-stabilized apartment downtown. While she had spent most of her early life pursuing life as an artist, the need for reliable health insurance drove her to take a corporate gig she didn't want a few years before Rob passed away. Now, she told me, she left the apartment only to go to work.

Ruth's chief complaint, during her first appointment, was insomnia. She was plagued by intrusive thoughts about her husband's last days, as he wasted away from the metastatic tumors that had invaded his brain. Over the next few months, as she opened up more to tell me about her past artistic career, I could see she was suffering from more than just grief. That box-to-box living was also taking its toll. When I first suggested that a trip out of the city might be beneficial, she balked a bit.

"What would I do by myself?" she asked. "It's not like being outside is going to cure me of missing Rob."

About six months after Ruth started coming to see me, my family and I headed back to Indiana for the summer. It was my daughter's first extended trip to see where I grew up—and we planned to help my parents out and let Greta enjoy all the benefits of nature during those warm months. I was also keeping up with my full roster of patients in my practice. Thanks to upgrades in internet connectivity, I could check in with patients like Ruth through video calls. With this new view into my country life, Ruth became more curious.

"Is that your farm behind you?" she asked. "Did I just hear a cow mooing?"

Yes and yes, I replied. The next week, Ruth wanted to know what we grew on the farm. We were no longer spending our time focusing on her grief and isolation. All of a sudden, she wanted to talk about the intricacies of the Indiana nightsong. As the sun set, the symphony of bird calls and tree frogs had captured Ruth's attention.

"It doesn't sound like that at all upstate," she said. "At least not that I remember."

When I mentioned that I found it interesting that Ruth kept talking about nature during our talks, both with regard to missing Rob, as well as what she missed most from her artistic pursuits, she grew quiet. I thought perhaps I had pushed her too far. But, by the next week, I was in for a surprise. Ruth excitedly told me about an impromptu trip thirty miles north of the city to Cold Spring, New York, to hike. She brought her camera along and started taking photographs. While she was a bit anxious about heading into the wild on her own, that first hike inspired a second. Then a third. Before long, she was taking regular trips to mountains and the beach. Within six months, she had done the unthinkable as a die-hard New Yorker: she bought a used Subaru Outback so she could head out of the city whenever the whim struck.

"There's just something about being outside that feels *right*," she said. "I feel so vibrant and alive. Something wakes up in me. And taking these photos has really put me back in touch with my creative side. I never thought I'd have that again without Rob."

There are all manner of things that can happen to bring undue stress into our lives. But when we deprive our brains of nature for prolonged periods of time, managing that stress becomes harder. The lights, the noise, the crowds—these are all environments that can put our physiological systems on high alert. It can exacerbate depression or anxiety symptoms. But we aren't doomed to live lives of stressful desperation. We always have the power to go outside. Nature is everywhere.

RETURN TO THE FOREST

Am I telling you it's time to move out of your city apartment and buy a ranch in the middle of Nowhere, Montana? No. (I mean, unless you really want to.) But cultivating Mental Fitness should involve increasing your exposure to the outdoors.

In my practice in New York City, many of my patients had a very different relationship with nature than I had growing up. While I helped my dad plant trees and weed the gardens, most of my patients thought of nature as just the weather—or a walk in the park. I couldn't help but notice, however, that when they left the city, often for a beach trip, they felt *different*. One patient, a young man in his early thirties, told me how surprised he was that the sound of the waves was so soothing.

"I relaxed for the first time in months," he told me. "I didn't even really want to go on the trip initially—but it was just unbelievable."

Others would wax poetic about the leaves upstate during the autumn months—or the sparkle of the snow in the sun when they headed to the mountains to ski. Being outside made them feel something different. It is not just that they unplugged, but that they plugged into something very healing.

While it would be all too easy to say this was simply a by-product of taking a much-needed break (and I'm sure that played a role), the latest research suggests that being outside is just good for mental health. Studies that compare the mental health of people who are regularly exposed to green space show that they have a reduced risk of depression and anxiety compared to those who stick to strictly urban environments. Other research suggests that people who have already been diagnosed with a mental health concern can see improvement in their symptoms when they regularly head outside—and some studies put the short-term results on par with tested talk therapy interventions. There are now dozens of mental health practitioners who prescribe outdoor time in green or blue spaces—a new field known as ecotherapy.

While it might not be practical to tell my patients to take more vacations, I can recommend they spend more time outside, taking walks in the park on nice days or taking some time on the weekends to explore the great nature opportunities outside the five boroughs of the city. As a country boy who had chosen New York City as my home for so many years, it felt somewhat strange to think that the place I had come from, rural America, might hold some of the secrets to my patients' mental health. But it was hard to ignore that it was what so many people I saw needed. Even more so when I realized that the patients who took me up on my suggestions to spend more time in the outdoors benefited tremendously. They were using that time in natural environments to boost their Mental Fitness.

THE SOOTHING SOUND OF NIGHTSONG

When we learned my wife was pregnant with our second child, we realized our small apartment in the West Village would no longer work for us. As we searched for a new place to live, I looked at each potential apartment with an eye toward an ideal home for a growing family. Going back to Indiana wasn't in the cards at that moment, but I thought we could swing two bedrooms, maybe three, and a place with lots of natural light and some outdoor space. We found a great two-bedroom on Ninety-Seventh Street just across the street from Central Park. It barely fit into our budget—and there were no park views—but I considered us lucky to be close to more than eight hundred acres of outdoor space.

The first night, as I started to fall asleep, I found myself roused by the familiar *bing-bong* of the nearby subway, quickly followed by the muffled voice announcing the arrival of the C train. Even with the windows closed, I heard train after train making their stop at the station on the corner. I wondered how I had missed this flaw when we looked at the apartment and immediately ordered a set of white noise machines for the apartment.

When summertime came around, we headed back to Indiana—it was the June just before our son Forrest's birth. After days spent playing outside, Greta would fall asleep immediately, tired out by all the fun. And as the evening stretched out before my wife and me, I found myself lulled into relaxation by the nightsong. All the bird and frog sounds that so captivated Ruth from afar became my family's nightly lullaby. While I would sometimes struggle to sleep in New York, I never had that problem back in Indiana.

As it turns out, nature sounds are soporific, meaning sleep-inducing.

When researchers played nature sounds, like the nightsong, to patients in the coronary care unit, they found that, like pure silence, they significantly improved sleep quality. The study participants reported longer sleep times and fewer nighttime wakings.

You've already heard me talk about the importance of sleep quality to Mental Fitness. When you can find ways to add some nightsong into your routine, whether through recordings, a night out camping under the stars, or an open window up in the mountains, you will be surprised how quickly your body—and your mind—quiet.

GETTING GROUNDED

Growing up in Indiana, I spent a good deal of time with my hands in the dirt. Not only would I help my parents with different chores around the farm, but I also had a little garden of my own. It was something I always enjoyed. The magic of watching something you planted from a seed grow into a full-fledged plant. The pride in harvesting tomatoes or lettuce—and then serving them for supper. When my family moved back to Indiana, I immediately started a new garden plot and spent a great deal of what little free time I had composting, building raised beds, and coaxing seedlings into good, wholesome food. It made me feel good.

My work in the dirt was also bolstering my mental health—in ways you might not expect.

The latest research shows that natural environments, including forests and beaches, fill the air with powerful molecules called negative ions. Negative ions are molecules with an abundance of electrons—hence the name—but, as it turns out, they play quite a positive role in brain health. Several research studies have shown that exposure to these molecules increases the production of serotonin, a neurotransmitter associated with mood regulation. In addition, people who are exposed more often to negative ions report better mood and mental health. While researchers aren't exactly sure *how* negative ions work this kind of mood magic, there's enough evidence to suggest that being outside in natural environments is neuroprotective—and can help improve mental health.

You also find these negative ions in the dirt itself. And when you partake in the act of "grounding" (sometimes called "earthing"), which is simply walking barefoot outdoors or getting your hands dirty in the garden, all those extra electrons can help bring balance to the body. Studies suggest that grounding can improve sleep, reduce stress, and even improve immune response. It's also been shown to improve mood. In fact, a 2015 study found that grounding, when compared to an intervention like grounding without any contact to the earth, significantly improved mood in individuals after a single hour. Other studies have shown that this simple act of touching the earth has powerful anti-inflammatory effects. Walking barefoot is one of my favorite aspects of life on the farm.

While not all of us can necessarily put a big garden plot outside our doors, there are ways to gain the benefits of grounding, even in an urban setting. You can fill a window box with your favorite flowers—or bring houseplants into your home. Today you can even find cool mini-garden setups that allow you to not only make contact with the dirt, but also grow healthy greens or veggies in a small galley kitchen.

It just goes to show that, when you are working to improve your Mental Fitness, you don't always have to go to nature—you can also bring nature to you.

Take Eskenazi Hospital in Indianapolis. Hospitals have long been known as sterile, loud, and stress-inducing places. It's definitely not a place where most go to relax. But with research studies showing that the presence of green space in hospitals leads to better patient outcomes, including shorter recovery times after surgery and less use of pain medication, not to mention lower stress ratings from both patients and staff, the hospital invested in creating the Commonground, an outdoor green space that acts at the hospital's entry point. The plaza has a fountain, lots of plants, and a weekly farmers' market for the hospital staff. Even patients who only have a view of this spot from their window benefit from it being nearby.

Mental Fitness asks each of us to be bold like the leaders of Eskenazi Hospital and to bring more nature into our experience. Take Jason, a young thirtysomething man who came to see me to help deal with his generalized anxiety disorder. He hated the outdoors. Absolutely *hated* it. Jason spent the majority of his off hours sitting on his couch playing video games. He didn't even like to venture out to grab dinner. He would just have takeout delivered to his front door. When during one of our sessions he expressed a desire for more human interaction, I asked him what was stopping him from heading outside to meet up with friends or engage in an activity where he might meet some new people.

"They are working on the brick facade of my building right now," he said quickly. "I don't want to breathe in all that dust."

A few weeks later, I suggested an outing again. This time Jason said he was worried that being out and about might cause his allergies to flare up. I might have thought that Jason was agoraphobic, but he had no qualms leaving his apartment each day and jumping on the subway to head to work. He just had no interest in being outside simply for the sake of being outside. It quickly became clear to me that if I couldn't convince Jason to go to happy hour with colleagues after work, he probably wouldn't go for a trip out to the beach or upstate. When I said as much, he laughed.

"Do I look like an outdoorsy guy to you?" he said. "I'm definitely not someone who is going to go camping."

But he was, apparently, open to sharing his home with a houseplant.

That Christmas, Jason's mother sent him a peace lily. She thought it would add a little warmth to his apartment, and, she added, they are nearly impossible to kill. For whatever reason, Jason took to the flower. He tended to it and even called it Lily, as if it were a roommate. In all honesty, it kind of was. Within a few months, he brought a few more plants home. They, too, all were given names—and a good bit of tender loving care from Jason. When I told him I was surprised he was enjoying taking care of these plants, he was circumspect.

"I like them," he said with a smile. "Taking care of them relaxes me. And, maybe it sounds a little funny to say this, but they are pretty good listeners."

Fast-forward another year and Jason's anxiety symptoms decreased significantly. He learned that his apartment building had a community garden space nearby. He started to meet up with several of his neighbors one weekend a month, planting tomatoes, basil, and some blooming perennials. What started as a little green in his own home led to him finding more time to spend outdoors, no camping required. It was a win for his overall mental health.

AN OUTDOOR PRESCRIPTION FOR MENTAL FITNESS

In Japan, where people live active, high-quality lives well into their golden years, many people engage in *shinrin-yoku*, or forest bathing. This practice, which became en vogue back in the 1980s, does not require a tent or even broken-in hiking boots. It's merely the act of walking in any natural environment, breathing deeply, and being consciously present in the space. Like the other studies examining the effects of nature on human physiology, researchers have found that *shinrin-yoku* is an incredible antidote to urban burnout and box-to-box living. Studies show that it is linked to improvements in blood pressure, immune function, and mood.

While you can find several different types of guided *shinrin-yoku* tours even on this side of the Pacific, you can obtain all the benefits of green spaces on your own. One of the best things about ecotherapy is that it takes only a little green-space boost to make a big impact. It can all start with a one-hour walk out of doors.

It's long been known that a good walk can help people manage stress. But, as it turns out, walking in a more natural setting can give you extra benefits. When researchers at Germany's Max Planck Institute compared magnetic resonance images (MRIs) of the brains of sixty-three people after they took a one-hour walk on a busy, urban street compared to one in the forest, they found that walking in the woods helped to keep stress regions of the brain, like the amygdala, on a more even keel. The deactivation in the amygdala was so pronounced that the researchers argue that a walk in the woods can act as a "preventive measure" to support mental and emotional well-being.

You don't even have to drive upstate to take that walk. You can head to your local park. And if just walking seems too boring, you can mix your time in green or blue spaces with other engaging activities. Join a local birding group. Go geocaching or play a game outside with your kids. Plan a picnic. Or follow Ruth's example. She's now joined an artistic collective that takes regular trips upstate. They hike, talk about the state of the world, and look to the forest or beach to provide a little extra artistic inspiration. You can also follow Jason's route to ecotherapy. Buy yourself a plant or become involved with a community garden. Take advantage of what the green and blue spaces near you have to offer.

Ecotherapy, whether you engage in grounding, gardening, or forest bathing, is a boon to Mental Fitness. Finding ways to connect with nature brings a sense of calm and meaning. It is also a great way to leave the hustle and bustle of modern life behind and just slow down. It reminds our nervous systems that we were built to do more than just get lost in our screens and stress. Healing the modern brain means giving the mind more of what it needs to thrive—and, in this case, that means a rest. Time spent in green and blue spaces can provide just that, and, as a result, lead to reduced inflammation, improved mood, and overall better mental health.

CLIMATE CHANGE AND MENTAL HEALTH

I would be remiss if I did not mention that climate change is doing more than damaging our environment—it is also disturbing our collective physical and mental health. The smoke from wildfires, mold from flooding events, and general anxiety from the latest climate change disaster are affecting the way we feel. It's why the American Psychological Association not only issued a 2017 report discussing the dangers of climate change on people's physical, mental, and community health, but also founded a Council on Climate Change to help mental health

practitioners understand the impacts of a warming planet—
and look for ways to help people who have been affected by
this ongoing problem.

I mention this because, as you think about the power
of Mother Nature to build Mental Fitness, it is imperative
that we also work to protect her. The growing amount of
climate change anxiety supports the idea that grounding is
an integral part of mental health. Being in nature can help
address the existential dread that can infiltrate the mind,
especially as we age. When we understand the fundamental
connection between mental health and the outdoors, we can
be more proactive about making the little changes that can
help curb climate disasters.

CHAPTER 10

Unburdening

Sofia had spent most of her life being her brother's keeper. Nicolas had been born with cerebral palsy, a congenital disease that affects motor function. While Nicolas could walk with the help of specially designed mobility aids, he had incredible difficulty with balance and often fell—leading to significant injuries. The worst happened when Nicolas was about eight years old. He slipped while trying to climb up some stairs, resulting in a compound fracture in his arm and a concussion. Unsurprisingly, Sofia's mother was very, very anxious about someone always keeping an eye on Nicolas. And with three other siblings in the house, that task most often fell to Sofia, the oldest.

"I really didn't mind that much. Nicolas has always been a joy," she said. "But I started to realize, probably by the time I was fifteen or so, that a lot of my mother's anxiety about him—whether he was okay, whether he was getting worse, whether he had friends at school, what life would be like for him once I graduated from high school—was rubbing off on me."

Sofia opted to go to university nearby so she could be close enough to help with Nicolas's care. But, as time went on, she realized her anxiety was increasing. And it wasn't only about Nicolas.

The anxiety was, as she described it, growing like a force field, and starting to engulf almost every other area of her life. She felt it most keenly when she started to date someone at school.

"At the start of my senior year, he started to talk about marrying after graduation and all I could think about was, 'How am I going to get married? Who is going to help with Nicolas?'" she said. "The guy was great—and he was great with Nicolas and my family, too—but the idea of moving on and starting a family of my own was just too much. It overwhelmed me. And the idea of having children of my own? It was just terrifying. The whole idea of it put me into a place where I could barely deal with him anymore."

Within a few weeks, the boyfriend was history. And, over the next decade, Sofia told me, she kept most of her relationships at arm's distance, too apprehensive to let anyone outside her immediate family get too close. Then, unexpectedly, she met a man she could see herself building a future with—but quickly realized that would be possible only if she could find a way to manage her anxiety. That's when she decided to make an appointment with me.

"I need to sort this out," she said. "What I'm doing just isn't working anymore—and I can't keep carrying all this worry and anxiety and old stuff around with me. It's going to scare away anyone worth keeping around."

From a distance, it is all too easy to understand where Sofia's anxiety had come from. In some ways, that level of anxiety may have even been beneficial to providing Nicolas the right kind of care. But it wasn't helping with Sofia's life *now*. The life outside her family home, with a career in business, and an eye on the future. The burden of all those old anxious feelings was interfering with her being able to connect, to grow, and to flourish in this new world where she now wanted to thrive. That, as you can imagine, was taking a toll on her overall mental health.

But it's important to understand that it's not just anxiety that can be a burden. Any unprocessed emotion, issue, or trauma can weigh us down. And many of us carry around old feelings or experiences that hinder our peace and well-being. We may have buried them deep (or at least think that we have), but cultivating Mental Fitness involves ensuring that we bring these different concerns to light. We must find ways to process and manage them so they don't disrupt our mental and physical health.

Mental Fitness requires that we find a way to unburden ourselves.

MODERN NARRATIVES AND TREATMENT PATTERNS

When you hear "mental health," what images spring to mind? Is it a comfortable-looking leather couch in an office filled with medical books? Is it a therapist, sitting across the room, his pen scratching on a yellow notepad as he says "Hmmm . . ." while you talk about your mother? Maybe you picture an array of medication commercials.

The modern context of mental health care, and the narratives surrounding therapy and treatment, have evolved radically in recent decades. But there remain inconsistencies, misconceptions, and vagaries that can make it difficult and confusing for those seeking help to obtain the information they need. So, let's take a look behind the curtain to see what we're doing now and—crucially—what's missing.

Let's say you're not feeling well mentally. You're tired. You have brain fog. No motivation. Getting out of bed is hard. Your thoughts are racing with worries. All of these symptoms line up with symptoms for depression or anxiety, so it's pretty clear-cut. However, statistics show that the majority of people suffering from such symptoms will not seek help. We see that people don't come in for treatment until something becomes a major problem. Sometimes even then, studies show that you're not overly likely to make an appointment with a psychiatrist or therapist, either. Surprisingly, ob-gyns are the doctors who are most likely to screen for mental health issues, followed by general family practitioners. And if they hear that you are experiencing some of these symptoms, they may offer you a prescription, or suggest that you follow up with a mental health professional or a psychiatrist like myself for some talk therapy.

Talk therapy works through, well, talking. That's what you're probably imagining when you think about mental health treatment. Tony Soprano in a room talking back and forth with his doctor, all in a way that advances the plot of season two. However, most talk therapy relationships between doctor and patient last on average just eight sessions. How long therapy should take really depends on the type of therapy, what a patient is struggling with, and what the goals of treatment are.

Psychotherapy or talk therapy is really near and dear to my heart both as a practitioner and as a patient. It was a tool I used myself starting in medical school as I worked to manage my stress and improve my mood. It helped me better understand my own mind—and how I approached different situations. Today, when I meet with patients I'm really focused on understanding more about who they are, hearing about the types of things they often don't discuss with other individuals, the inner workings of their minds, what their fears are, and what their dreams are. Talk therapy, at its core, is finding words for feelings. It allows us to learn to better express and communicate our inner world to other people and make sense of all the emotions that all humans have. In psychotherapy, we can help patients address fundamental issues around self-esteem and confidence, or deal with difficult relationships, sorting out how you want to proceed, or how best to communicate with your partner or with your boss. Psychotherapy also helps us come into some resolution with some of the conflicts that all people have, between our hopes and our dreams, and the realities of what our life is. Psychotherapy really gives you a frame or space to better explore and understand who you are. With Sofia, talk therapy gave her a safe space to better understand the roots of her anxiety—and how to better manage it so it wasn't an impediment to her future relationships.

Understanding the therapeutic process isn't always easy. There are many different kinds of psychotherapy—and different practitioners take different approaches. But what I'd like to make clear is that there is ample evidence to show that when you work with a clinician that you fit well with, someone you can be open and honest with, you are likely to show an improvement in your depression and anxiety symptoms.

Unfortunately, talk therapy isn't always an option for everyone. The modern world—and modern health care—don't always make it easy for us to unburden ourselves.

UNBURDENING OURSELVES IN THE MODERN WORLD

Modern human beings are supposed to be strong, capable, and impervious to trauma, whether it's trauma with a big *T* or little *t*. What doesn't kill you makes you stronger, right? But even if we want to deal with the things that have happened or are happening to us, it can be a challenge. To start, as noted by Canadian physician and author Gabor Maté, our society is simply not set up in a way to meet basic human developmental needs, let alone provide us with the support we need to recover from trauma. Second, the United States is experiencing an unprecedented shortage in behavioral health therapists—and the lack of licensed psychologists, licensed social workers, and psychiatrists means that many people are having to wait a ridiculously long time for even a rudimentary talk therapy session. And, if you can find an appointment, chances are you are going to have to pay out of pocket for it. Even the White House has sounded the alarm on the economic burden involved in getting suitable mental health care in America. It's a huge problem that makes accessing mental health care an ongoing challenge for people with limited resources.

Is it any wonder, with these factors at play, that we've gotten so adept at burying our feelings? We're not supposed to have them in the first place. If we admit that we do, we often have nowhere to go to deal with them. Instead we pretend that if we keep them below the surface, we can just safely ignore them. And sometimes, for a while, we can. Except our nervous systems won't allow us to go on like that indefinitely. Those feelings have a habit of creeping up when we least expect them to. And they can wreak havoc on our relationships and experiences if we aren't careful. That's why unburdening needs to be more of a priority.

Unfortunately, the very things that make it so hard to unburden ourselves are the very reasons why it is even more imperative that we find ways to do so. We all have our baggage—you can't go through life without acquiring some—and so finding ways to be more aware of how your past may be affecting the way you navigate your present is important. Also, adopting small strategies to unburden yourself will allow you to get to a point where your previous experiences won't interfere with you taking control of your future.

That starts with understanding the power of adverse experiences.

UNDERSTANDING THE POWER OF ADVERSE EXPERIENCES

In the 1980s, Vincent Felitti, MD, founded the Department of Preventive Medicine for Kaiser Permanente, an integrated managed health care organization in California. The department was working on a new obesity treatment program to help patients lose weight and improve their physical health. The program was working, too. Many people in the program were successfully shedding pounds with new evidence-based interventions. But much to Dr. Felitti's surprise and dismay, many of the patients, despite their progress, were dropping out of the program and immediately gaining the weight back. When he and his colleagues reached out to those patients to try to understand why, they discovered something shocking: the onset of obesity for the vast majority of the program's dropouts was linked to childhood adverse experiences, including physical and sexual abuse.

Felitti kept hearing the same kinds of stories over and over again—and after reporting it to other doctors at a National Obesity Meeting in 1990, he connected with Robert Anda, MD, a researcher at the Centers for Disease Control and Prevention. Felitti and Anda would go on to conduct the largest investigation of adverse childhood experiences (ACEs) and how it affected health and well-being in later life using data from over 17,000 participants from across the United States. They discovered that when children are exposed to ACEs, which can include child abuse, neglect, domestic violence, substance abuse of family members, or other traumatic stressors like divorce, an incarcerated parent, mental illness, or bullying, the risk of developing later mental or physical health issues significantly increases. What's more, the more ACEs a child is exposed to, the more their risk of chronic health issues goes up—as does the risk of early death.

Sofia did not think of her childhood as a traumatic one—and, as it turns out, when asked directly, many of the people surveyed in the ACEs study, unless they were exposed to the worst of the worst abuse, didn't think so, either. Yet some of Sofia's experiences fall into the ACE categories. Because Nicolas required so much care, her emotional needs were often overlooked. Though as an adult, she completely understood why it had to be that way—her mother had only so much time and energy—she admitted she often felt emotionally neglected when she was younger. But she had to learn to deal with it. She quickly learned that she had to be another "grown-up" in the household when most of her friends were still able to be children. It was necessary to help the household run.

Sofia's mother's anxiety was pervasive, too, to the point where Sofia once described it to me as "infecting the household." That, too, can be considered an ACE. Even if you were not subjected to the horrors of physical or sexual abuse, there may be issues from your childhood or upbringing that may seem on their face benign but may still require a little processing for you to embrace optimal Mental Fitness.

For example, I have another client, Patrick, who is incredibly uncomfortable when it comes to personal finance, even though he has a great and well-paying tech job. He finds himself very uncomfortable having conversations with his wife about their household budget. He refuses to look at or pay any bills. When his family recently decided to renovate their kitchen, he went out of his way to avoid visiting the bank to sign the paperwork for a home equity loan—making his wife quite angry as he missed appointment after appointment. When I asked him why he was so reticent to deal with money matters, he at first dodged the question.

"Isn't it my job to make the money?" he said. "I'm relying on my wife to manage it. I don't see why I have to be involved. I'm busy enough with my work."

But as we talked more over the coming months, I learned that Patrick came from a rather impoverished background. His father had struggled to hold down a job throughout his childhood—and his mother was always taking in extra work to try to make ends meet. He remembered, at one point, his mother dressing him and his sisters up in their Sunday best to go down to the bank. They had fallen behind on their mortgage payments and his mother was asking for some grace until she could make up the difference. It was, he told me, deeply humiliating and not the only time his mother used the family to plead for financial leniency. All of a sudden, the idea of avoiding a trip to the bank to sign some loan paperwork didn't seem so strange anymore.

"Does your wife know about that?" I asked him.

"She doesn't want to know that stuff."

"It might help her understand you better—and why you can be somewhat reticent about engaging about the finances."

It took some time, but we started to talk about ways that he could communicate about money. But exposing himself to it a little bit at a time—a small bill here, a bank statement there—he learned to be more comfortable about the topic. And to understand that his nervous system was reacting to *then*, not now.

EXPOSURE AND RESPONSE PREVENTION

All of us are subject to recurrent worries or associations that may drive us to act oddly at times. It's worth being aware of them, and taking the time to understand where those feelings are coming from. If you find yourself going back to a moment in time, kind of like the needle on a record player becoming stuck on a particular track, playing it over and over again, that's a hint that you may have something that you need to work out.

For Patrick, it was financial stuff. For another patient, David, it was all about dating. After leaving a nearly decade-long relationship, David had serious social anxiety about jumping back into the dating pool. We talked about it for a good while. We examined his fears, and why he felt so nervous about getting back out there. We even went over what he should write in his online dating profile. But there comes a point when it's time to stop talking and start doing—and just acknowledge that, especially at first, dating is going to be uncomfortable.

Let's face it: life, sometimes, will be uncomfortable. If you wait for everything to be comfortable, you'll never accomplish anything. That is part of the basis of exposure and response prevention (ERP) therapy, a type of behavioral therapy that is often used to treat obsessive-compulsive disorder (OCD) and anxiety. The idea is simple: you gradually expose people to situations that they feel somewhat reticent about in a safe environment to help provide them with coping skills to better deal with it.

With David, our ERP approach started fairly simply. I asked him to send someone who looked interesting on his dating app a message. While it did make him a little anxious, we talked about those feelings, why he was experiencing them, and how to manage them. When he felt like he was at a point where he could comfortably message people on the dating site, we moved on to Step Two: setting up an afternoon coffee date. The idea of ERP is to build up exposure to something that may be causing you some anxiety, recognize why those feelings may be there, and work through them. While at first David found the exercise slightly terrifying, he kept at it. Now, six months later, he is swimming in dates. And he knows that he needs to keep meeting new people until he meets someone whom he feels he can commit to.

Most of the time, ERP is done strictly with a therapist to coach you. But, more and more, I see friends and family members doing their own form of ERP to lessen the load of their baggage. One friend had a speech impediment growing up and was bullied mercilessly for it. He has always struggled with public speaking. Recently he made a career change that has required him to do more in-person presentations. He realized that to make the most of his new job, he was going to have to figure out how to move past his fear of public speaking. He decided to join Toastmasters International, a nonprofit educational organization that helps people build public-speaking skills.

"I went for months and did not say a word, Drew," he told me. "I'd go and sit at the table and just listen. But, finally, I decided I needed to try. I walked up there and gave my little speech. I tried to incorporate all the tips and tricks they had talked about in the meetings. And when I finished—you know, I could learn to like all that applause."

Like anything else in mental health, there's not one way to unburden. You can find what works for you. For some, that will be going to a mental health counselor. For others, that may mean finding that Toastmasters group or finally having an open and honest conversation with their partner about why a particular topic can be so off-putting. But it all starts with self-awareness. That understanding that there are some people and situations that put your nervous system on high alert—and may require you to take a step back, take a deep breath (or ten), and do what's necessary to embody those circumstances with understanding and grace.

Two years after entering therapy, Sofia's anxiety is well managed. She married that great guy—and they are expecting their first child. Every once in a while she has a flash of worry, but she has an arsenal of tools to help bring her nervous system back to baseline. Taking the time to unburden herself wasn't easy, but it was integral in helping her promote her own Mental Fitness.

It will, no doubt, be just as integral in helping you to promote yours, too.

CHAPTER 11

Purpose

It felt as though Maia had worked her whole life for this single moment: her residency match. She had always been a high achiever, even during her elementary school years. She was always on the honor roll, took home top prizes at debate competitions and science fairs, and was invited to participate in invite-only academic camps each summer. She graduated at the top of her class from high school with the goal of going to an elite university. She ended up having her choice of three Ivy League schools—and selected the one with the most decorated premed program. After finishing her bachelor's degree, she was immediately accepted at a prestigious medical school, where she once again graduated with honors. She had dedicated eight years of her life to higher education, spending most of her time in the library or the hospital. The culmination of those years led her to this very moment. Sitting in her small apartment on a Monday morning, she repetitively refreshed her laptop to see if she had been granted entrance to the next step she would need to take to become a surgeon: a place in a highly competitive surgical residency program in New York City.

"My parents were on FaceTime supporting me," she said. "And when the results came up and showed that I matched, they were so excited. My dad was yelling how proud he was. My mom was crying with joy. And I just felt . . . nothing."

That lack of feeling is why her parents sent her to see me. They could not understand why Maia wasn't over the moon with her most recent accomplishment. But, as she and I talked, it was clear that so much of what she had accomplished over the years had been spurred by extrinsic motivation. Meaning that she worked as hard as she did to please her parents, her teachers, and her community, but not necessarily to please herself. Early on, people expected her to do great things. After spending so much time and effort to achieve what was supposed to be her "dream," she realized she was at an impasse. She did not want to join this residency program. She did not want to be a surgeon. The problem was, she was not sure what she wanted to do. After following everyone else's lead for so long, Maia realized she lacked purpose.

As a physician, I know there are many reasons why people decide to pursue a career in medicine. Some are called to the healing arts because they want to do work where they can improve the lives of others. But there are others who end up in the field because they follow one ultrahigh-achieving step after the other. Far too often, once they reach the top of that achievement staircase, they look down and aren't quite sure how they ended up there. It's more common than you might think, and the pattern doesn't just occur in medicine. You see it in other top fields, too. Unfortunately, many lack the self-awareness to realize there may be an issue. They just keep going along as they've always done, even if the work they are doing is not a good fit. But others, like Maia, do realize something is amiss. And believe me, she is far from the only person who has ended up sitting across from me, wondering how they've ended up living the particular life they are currently inhabiting. They are looking for *more*, some kind of driving force to help guide them forward.

They are seeking a sense of purpose.

No doubt, if you've spent any time browsing the self-help aisles or thinking about self-improvement, you are familiar with the idea of purpose—and why it's so important to living a good life. Transcendentalist poet Ralph Waldo Emerson once wrote, "The purpose of life is not to be happy. It is to be useful, to be honorable, to be compassionate, to have it make some difference that you have lived and lived well." I've always liked that quote—though it isn't exactly a how-to guide to finding a way to live well. So, if pressed, I would say that, at its simplest, purpose is just a central, organizing life aim. A sense of direction or a setting of intention, if you will. Austrian psychiatrist Viktor Frankl, in his book *Man's Search for Meaning*, believed that finding one's purpose was a driving force in living a meaningful life.

In many circles, purpose is cast as a spiritual or religious concept. It certainly can be, if religion or spirituality is something you rely on as a compass to guide you as you make decisions, interact with others, and make your way about the world. But purpose can be just as beneficial for those of us who do not have the same kind of spiritual framework. In those cases, it's often a cohesive sense of direction and serving something larger than the self that helps to give your life a sense of value and meaning. And it, too, can help guide your actions and decisions. You just don't have to attribute those values to a particular dogma. Here's the thing, though: with or without a particular doctrine or denomination, research has found that having a purpose helps to support better mental and physical health.

To start, purpose appears to help increase longevity. A group of epidemiologists at the Boston University School of Public Health, Harvard T. H. Chan School of Public Health, and Lee Kum Sheung Center for Health and Happiness at the University of British Columbia decided to look at data from the Health and Retirement Study, a unique data set of more than 13,000 individuals over the age of fifty years from across the United States. At the start of the study, the participants were all given a metric called the Ryff Psychological Wellbeing Scale. That metric includes seven questions regarding purpose, with statements like *Some people wander aimlessly through life, but I am not one of them* and *I don't have a good sense of what I'm trying to accomplish in my life.* Respondents rated each statement using a 6-point Likert scale, where 1 means "strongly disagree" and 6 equals "strongly agree." The responses were then put together to create a mean sense-of-purpose score. When the researchers analyzed the data, they found that having a higher average purpose score was associated with a lower mortality risk, from any cause. This, the authors suggested, may mean purpose could be a "health asset" for people, especially as they grow older.

Purpose doesn't just have benefits for physical health, as it turns out. Australian researchers looked at the relationship between purpose and mental health—particularly depression and anxiety diagnoses—through a meta-analysis of studies in the scientific literature. Across a wide range of studies, they found that when individuals reported having a greater purpose in life, they were less likely to have depression and anxiety. Psychologists have argued that purpose may act as a buffer for people and help them be more resilient.

There's also some evidence to suggest it may provide a literal biological buffer of sorts. The Midlife in the United States Neuroscience (MIDUS) project, which looks at the effects of midlife on the brain, found that having a sense of purpose is associated with distinct changes that appear to promote resilience and overall brain health. Researchers from the University of Wisconsin–Madison, using diffusion-weighted magnetic resonance imaging (MRI), which allows a detailed look at microstructural features in the brain, showed that people who report living with purpose have increased white matter, which is associated with better memory and signal conduction. They also show healthier activity in the hippocampus, the region of the brain associated with learning and memory. Still other studies have shown that purpose is linked to increased cognitive reserve, which, as we discussed in Chapter 8, also plays a key role in overall Mental Fitness.

The MIDUS project also found that purpose also helps people better manage day-to-day stressors—you know, all those little daily annoyances that can sometimes drag you down. Even on stressful days, individuals with a sense of purpose report better mood and fewer physical symptoms related to stress compared to people without it. Other studies have shown that even in young people, purpose acts as a buffer during hard times, like the COVID-19 pandemic or the great recession in Greece, to help people envision brighter days ahead.

WHERE DO I FIND MY PURPOSE?

By now, no doubt, you, like me, are sold on the perks of having a sense of purpose. But you may be wondering how, exactly, you find one if you don't already have one in your possession. As someone who has, from time to time, had to take a step back and take a hard look at the guiding forces in my own life, I know it's not always easy to find this interior navigational system. Purpose evolves like the rest of us, over time and often as we reflect on powerful events in our lives.

Philosophers would tell you that the human need to derive purpose is part of the brain's need to make sense of the world around us. That makes a lot of sense to me. The brain, after all, has to process an awful lot of information. Whenever we can add some kind of filter that helps it sort the wheat from the proverbial chaff, we can help it work a lot more efficiently. I think the brain's desire to have this kind of additional perceptual sieve may be another reason why so many of us struggle to find our own sense of purpose. The world, at times, can seem like a pretty terrible place. And as we consume terrible news story after terrible news story, deal with unprocessed trauma, and generally deal with an environment that seems littered with danger, it can sometimes be challenging to believe there's a point to, well, anything.

The modern world—and the introduction of modern technology—means that we know just how vast the world is and how awful people can be to one another. We are distracted by the sheer enormity of what's around us, and between the doom-scrolling, the attempts to keep up with the Joneses, and the general fear of missing out (FOMO), it can sometimes be hard to figure out where we should be focusing our energy. That can lead to a serious feeling of inertia—it may seem like there's no place where any amount of effort will make a difference. But it's important to mention that there's something else the modern world is doing to us that interferes with us finding our purpose. These days, too many of us spend the majority of our time focused out instead of in.

As Maia and I spoke more, it became very clear that most of her life was lived for the approval of others. This went beyond academic achievement. Even her social life tended to revolve around what others thought was best for her. She dated people who belonged to the same social and religious organizations that her parents did. Even when she went off to school, she gravitated to those same types of groups. At the time, she would have told you they felt safe and welcoming, but now, she said, she realized that they were just easier—and would elicit fewer questions and judgment from her family.

"What would you have done differently, do you think?"

"I don't know."

"Well, if you don't want to do this residency, what do you want? What lights you up about life?"

Maia was silent for several moments.

"I don't know if I ever really asked myself that question," she said. "In fact, I'm not sure *anyone* has ever asked me that question. I know what my parents wanted for me. I know what my teachers thought I was capable of. I knew what I was supposed to do. But what I want? That's something, I think, I need to start focusing on."

I agreed. Because, while it is not always easy or readily apparent, what one's purpose may be—and there is no one-size-fits-all approach to finding it—it is a vital component to brain health and overall well-being. So, as a result, cultivating Mental Fitness involves finding yours.

FIND YOUR PURPOSE, FIND YOUR PATH

Purpose is something that comes up a lot with many of my patients—and, given its benefits to health and well-being, it's something well worth talking about. But even I must admit it's a pretty heavy subject. And, as I try to distill down the advice I give my patients, I would like to caution you to filter what I say through your own lens. You should always adapt my recommendations to your own specific goals and circumstances. As I already said, there is no one-size-fits-all approach to purpose. Some of you will find glimmers of purpose through your religious institutions or spiritual practices. Others will find a path forward through acts of service or playing to your strengths. Still others will find that inner direction by really doubling down on self-awareness or looking to mentors or role models. Maybe your way to purpose involves a combination of all of the above.

But where I suggest everyone starts is with a single question: *What can I do to live a life that I enjoy more?*

It may seem, at first glance, a very simple question. Maybe even a somewhat selfish and hedonistic one. But at the end of the day, the answer to this question is where your purpose—whatever it may be—resides. This is how you live a life with meaning. This is how you live a life that you want to embrace fully.

Maia couldn't tell me, at first, what she wanted most out of life. But she could tell me what she did *not* want. She did not want a career in surgery. She did not want to continue in a fast-paced, super-competitive career. But when the conversation moved toward what she could do to live a life that she enjoyed more, she had a lot more to say.

"I really love working with patients. One of the things that really bores me about surgery is that you don't get to really spend any real time talking with patients. You meet them, you do the procedure, you do a quick follow-up, but they always have so many other issues that you aren't in a position to address," she said.

As we talked more about what she enjoyed about medical school, she kept telling me incredible stories about her geriatrics rotation. It was clear that Maia really loved working with the elderly population and helping them with their physical and mental needs. It didn't take long for her to realize that she could stay in medicine in this kind of role. It would be something she would not only enjoy but would also be a way for her to feel she could provide the kind of holistic care for patients that would make a real difference in their lives. But changing medical specialties is no easy feat. It would require more time and training. Over the following months, Maia received a lot of pushback, and not just from her family, but also her mentors at medical school. It required her to take a step back and do a lot of soul-searching about what she really wanted.

The search for purpose is not always straightforward—or even linear. The things we think we desperately want aren't always as fulfilling as we think they should be (or as fulfilling as our parents think they should be). It can be challenging and complicated to look deep inside and figure out what really motivates us. But it's worth the time and effort.

So, as you ask yourself what you can do to live a life you enjoy more, I'd offer a few more pieces of advice. First, focus on the process that you enjoy. As I've listened to my patients find their sense of purpose, it seems to revolve around a process. Some love negotiating. Others adore watching their students learn new math concepts. I lose track of time when nurturing plants, animals, and people. Maia was drawn to the process of exploring her patients' complex medical problems more than the controlled, circumscribed process of performing surgery. Find your process to find your purpose. I bet it will lead you to just the right place.

Second, your purpose does not have to be a big, all-encompassing thing. People often think that purpose has to be something like "saving the world" or "eliminating greenhouse emissions." These are noble pursuits, to be sure. But so is being a trusted, reliable neighbor or a present parent. You need to find the purpose that is going to guide you in your daily life.

Third, your purpose can, and likely will, change over time. Like anything else in life, it's going to be somewhat dynamic. Finally, your purpose isn't always going to be immediately clear. This can be very frustrating and upsetting. For many, including myself, determining your path sometimes requires taking a pause in these challenging periods. Take that time to think about where you are, where you enjoy putting your time and energy in service of something. Provided you are looking within, and listening to what you need, you should be able to figure out what you need to guide you. But the answers may not always come up instantly. Unfortunately, they rarely do. You deserve some time to think about where your efforts have led to feelings of fulfillment, connection, and calm. A life dedicated to Mental Fitness requires you to make space in your life for meaning.

ABOUT FOLLOWING YOUR PASSION

There's no lack of books, podcasts, and social media influencers out in the world who will encourage you to follow your passion—and tell you that your passions are an integral part of your greater purpose. I feel a little differently than most when it comes to "passions." Mainly, that, generally speaking, most passions tend to burn fast and furious—and eventually lead to burnout.

Once again, your purpose doesn't have to be a sweeping, compendious thing. In my experience, the most meaningful purpose—

and, by that I mean, the types of purpose that offer the most direction, resilience, and gratification—is really quite small and personal. There's that old saying: if you want to change the world, start in your own backyard. I think purpose works on a similar scale. Whether you are looking for that central, organizing aim to direct you personally, professionally, in your relationships, in your community, or in any other way, you want to start looking for it within your own circle. The more I think about setting my own intentions in life—and the more I speak to patients like Maia and others—the more I believe purpose is really about repairing the broken relational patterns in our lives that prevent us from creating and maintaining connections with others. When we can find the space and acceptance to be ourselves, and be open about what we want and need. When we can help those around us feel safe and welcome to do the same.

The truth is, purpose is, at best, an enigmatic concept. And I can't tell you what your purpose is any more than you can tell me what mine is. But if you keep returning to the question, as I do, *What can I do to live a life I enjoy more?*, I think it becomes easier to figure out how to get there.

One way to start is, as they taught us in residency, to "follow the affect." As we trained to become psychiatrists, our mentors taught us that often what is most important is not *what* our patients tell us, but the feelings with which they express it. When their words come with a lot of emotion, it's time to pay attention. I would argue that, as you consider your purpose, it's worthwhile for you to follow for affect, too. What do you do in your life that brings you feelings of fulfillment and pleasure? When we have clarity about our purpose, we have those feelings. We are more decisive about our values— and our goals. As you search for your purpose, look at the things in your life that bring you peace and direction. Perhaps they come to you being part of a spiritual institution. Maybe you feel that way when you volunteer with a particular organization. Or maybe they are most present when you are working toward specific goals at work or being with your family.

So many people search for purpose like it is out there *somewhere.* That it will just magically appear out of the ether. In my experience, both in working with patients and in my own life, purpose is most often found within the confines of your daily life—in the everyday activities right in front of you. For example, it may seem like, as a physician, my purpose is obvious: heal the sick. But I've gotten much more mileage out of encouraging people to creatively explore how to cultivate Mental Fitness in new and creative ways. Whether I'm in the clinic, or out hiking with a friend deep in the woods, I feel most alive with creative mental exploration.

That said, for far too long, we've associated purpose with lofty professional goals or religious pursuits. And it's not that it can't be those things—it absolutely can be, and may be for you. But it may also be something far simpler. Seeing Maia now, in a geriatrics fellowship, where she, somewhat ironically, helps older patients find their purpose as they embrace their golden years, shows me that it can be something small and beautiful that gives your life meaning in unexpected ways.

Purpose is a core tenet of Mental Fitness because we are here not just to exist "symptom-free." We are here to contribute to the greater joy and beauty of the planet. And once you define your path toward this tenet, the more power you have to transform your struggles to solace. So, look inward, build on what you've already learned about a healthy brain, and continue to build on an already growing foundation of Mental Fitness . . . *with purpose.*

Building a More Resilient Brain

Ian, a hospital administrator in his forties, didn't have a specific complaint in mind when he came to see me. He had a certain sense of ennui, he said, and like many men of his age, worried that his concentration wasn't what it should be. And while he couldn't quite put his finger on what was wrong, he was quite certain what would put it right: psychedelic medicine.

"I keep reading about magic mushrooms and ketamine. They seem to be game changers," he said. "I've already tried a couple of different antidepressants. And while SSRIs did wonders for my sister, they just made me feel spaced-out."

He had heard that my clinic offered ketamine-assisted psychotherapy. With all the buzz about psychedelics and mental health, Ian hoped he would be a good candidate for what the *New York Times* had dubbed the "psychedelic revolution." Despite the fact that he didn't meet the criteria for a mental health diagnosis, he hoped that a ketamine "journey" would help him feel, well, better. The way he thought he should feel.

I've now been a psychiatrist for twenty-five years. I started in the hallways of Columbia University, where the so-called bible of psychiatry, the modern *Diagnostic and Statistical Manual of Mental*

Disorders (*DSM*), was first written, and so many discoveries about the brain were made. Over the years, I've borne witness to remarkable advances in the way we understand and treat mental health. And I've treated patients across a variety of settings, from major academic medical center inpatient units to community mental health centers to my own private practice.

Being on the frontiers of mental health has provided me with a profound sense of wonder about what is possible when it comes to brain health. But it has also given me a healthy dose of skepticism. And while I find myself optimistic about the potential of psychedelic-assisted therapy—so much so that I've now been trained to administer it myself—I know that I'm standing at yet another frontier of psychiatric medicine.

As a therapist, I want to be sure that I have access to every tool available to help my patients feel better. Today, the latest psychopharmacology research suggests that psychedelic drugs, or psychoactive compounds that can affect changes in perception, mood, and cognitive processes, have significant therapeutic potential for mental health conditions ranging from depression to post-traumatic stress disorder (PTSD).

Studies show that compounds like lysergic acid diethylamide (LSD), psilocybin (the active component in magic mushrooms), ketamine, and dimethyltryptamine (DMT) have significant clinical potential, especially when paired with psychotherapy. In a 2021 randomized clinical trial, researchers from Johns Hopkins University found that two psilocybin sessions, paired with psychotherapy, led to a seventy percent remission rate in the study participants. That's huge.

While each of these drugs works a little differently in the brain, many researchers liken their effects to a brain "reset." The drugs stimulate a special serotonin receptor, which helps put the brain into grow mode and helps each neuron to increase its synaptic connections. All these new and unwieldy connections, researchers argue, have a profoundly disorganizing effect on the brain. They also explain the main side effects of these drugs: the hallucinations, the out-of-body experiences, and profoundly "ineffable" experiences.

This same "reset" has made psychedelics such popular party drugs, but they can also provide therapists with tools to help patients more easily get in touch with unconscious traumas or barriers otherwise inaccessible during talk therapy. We can then work through them together so patients can move forward. I want to be clear: Psychedelics are not a panacea. They can come with often underappreciated risks. But they can be of great assistance to people who are struggling with serious mental health conditions, including depression, anxiety, PTSD, and even substance use disorders. Especially those who have not found relief with other pharmaceuticals or therapeutics.

I can understand why Ian was interested in psychedelics. He wanted, as he put it, "to feel more alive again." He hoped that ketamine could help with that. Certainly I understand that to some extent my job, if I'm doing it right, is to help people bolster their mental health so they never receive a mental health diagnosis.

I believe in the psychedelic revolution in psychiatry, to a point. In the months since I first trained to provide ketamine-assisted therapy, I've started a clinic and guide patients and groups in this process. I know there is a place for it with some patients. But, after experiencing my own ketamine journeys, and helping dozens of patients go through their own, I've realized psychedelics alone don't provide the answer to our mental health challenges. At best they seem to provide a trigger for deeper work, some symptom relief, and an enhanced sense of connection and spirituality for some. It should be understood that they are not the cure-all or quick fix that so many people hope they will be. The more I learn about the power of psychedelic-assisted therapy, the more I see that the people who benefit the most from it—or any type of therapy, really—are those who are already regularly engaging in multiple activities that promote healing in the brain. Ian was not the first person to come to me hoping to find relief with the help of psychedelic medicine. And he won't be the last. Yet the more I learn about psychedelic-assisted therapy—and there is still much to learn—the more I understand: with or without the help of medication, true brain reset comes from embracing the core tenets of Mental Fitness—and doing so, in some manner, each and every day.

TACKING TENETS TOGETHER

There's great dynamism in taking care of your brain. Intentional acts that promote self-awareness, nutrition, movement, sleep, connection, engagement, grounding, unburdening, and purpose can all counter the stressful effects of the modern world. The best part is that no drugs—hallucinogen or otherwise—are required. Healing the modern brain is all within your power. All you have to do is start adopting some Mental Fitness tenets in your own life.

I'm here to tell you, you can start small. I encourage you to do so. You now understand how and why the core tenets of Mental Fitness are so important to your overall health and well-being. But how you implement the lifestyle changes that promote them is entirely up to you. I'm not advocating for a total lifestyle overhaul. There's no need to overwhelm yourself. You can simply pick one tenet, one action to support that tenet, and then build from there.

Remember Ruth? Well into her sixties, she came to me to address issues with grief, anxiety, and persistent insomnia. We spent months engaged in the therapeutic process and, while she was making some progress, she really began to blossom after she started heading upstate to hike again. One change, making time to return to the outdoors, had a host of unexpected Mental Fitness perks. She reaped all the benefits of *shinrin-yoku*, or forest bathing, by heading out of the city to enjoy some greenery. She was hiking, which brought all the advantages of movement. The combined effects of exercise and grounding helped improve her sleep, putting all those intrusive thoughts at bay. And as she increased her visits to the forests, mountains, and beaches, she engaged with her photography. Finding ways to be more creative is a way to build cognitive reserve.

Ruth was not doomed to a life of stressful desperation. And neither are you.

Ronnie, who struggled with profound loneliness as an empty-nester, found similar relief when he started to think about ways to connect with others. A long-held passion for the Pittsburgh Steelers, mixed with a little courage, brought him into contact with other sports fans in similar life situations. That led to new and interesting social outlets—and the ability to build some deep friendships. But Ronnie didn't stop at building connections. As he's gotten older, he has realized the importance of staying sharp. He and his friends are not just heading out to watch football games anymore. They have also formed a formidable trivia team named Bradshaw's Brains. They play weekly, and often hang out to quiz each other on sports stats and movie quotes.

Then there's Maia, who, after years of pursuing a challenging career in surgery, found her true calling in geriatric medicine. By finding her actual purpose, instead of going through the motions in a job that didn't really appeal to her, she opened up her life to new social connections. She slept better, ate better, and had time to go to her favorite yoga classes. And she could make space for the things in life that made her feel good. It was a game changer.

That's one of the best things about the core tenets of Mental Fitness. They create a cascade of benefits that build on one another. Once you make a lifestyle change to affect one tenet, you'll quickly see how it can influence the others—often without you having to expend all that much extra effort. Spend some time on self-awareness and you'll be able to identify the places where you can most easily make some lifestyle tweaks to promote brain health. Add a daily walk to increase your movement or make some nutrient-dense ingredient swaps in your favorite meals and you'll soon notice that you are sleeping better. Join an exercise class or book club and achieve the double whammy of connection and engagement. Or, alternatively, start volunteering to build your sense of purpose—and you'll meet people with similar values whom you want to spend time with. Over time, you'll see how the different tenets combine in effective and exponential ways to improve your health and well-being—and help you lead a happier, more fulfilling life.

Pick a tenet, any tenet. Decide to make a change. See it through. You'll be surprised where it may take you—and the kind of resilience that will follow.

IT'S TIME FOR A MENTAL FITNESS REVOLUTION

I've pointed to many things in the modern world that take their toll on the brain—devices, toxins, ultraprocessed foods—but there is another stressor that we all face, no matter where or how we live our lives: uncertainty and change. My parents, back in Indiana, are now in their eighties. They are still living on the farm, and still desire to be independent. But they are going to need different things from me moving forward. I'm going to have to adapt.

Then there's my kids. My daughter is entering the teen years, with my son following closely behind. She tells me that a smartphone is a necessity—without it, she'd be socially isolated. Even with all the known concerns of teens and screens, I can't keep this device from her, any more than I can keep her apart from the rest of the modern world. Just as I'm navigating new territory as a son, I'm doing the same as a parent. Once again, I'm going to need flexibility and resilience for what I'm told—for what I know—will be an emotional and bumpy ride. And as I think about how to proceed, I keep coming back to this: my job is to keep working on my Mental Fitness. By being in the strongest mental shape possible, I can do my best to meet the moment and be what is needed for my loved ones. And because Mental Fitness has helped me deepen my emotional connections, I know I have my wife Lucy's support when I waver. All this is to say, we don't build Mental Fitness alone.

The world is complicated. Lives are complex. Relationships aren't always easy. And, much as we would like to control these things, mold them to our liking, that's not how it works. We cannot change the modern world, or the people who inhabit it. All we can do is control how we respond to it. That begins with building the kind of habits that will make our brains as healthy and resilient as possible. As I parent up and parent down in the coming years, I hope to model those habits so the people I love the most can learn how to cultivate Mental Fitness, too.

As I said at the start of the book, the brain is complicated. And given the breadth and scope of its job, it should be. But despite its complexity, caring for it really is quite simple. It's not always easy. But it is straightforward.

That's why I'm calling for a revolution. A Mental Fitness revolution. Healing the modern brain comes from embracing the core tenets of Mental Fitness—whether you have been diagnosed with a mental health condition or are, like so many of us today, just struggling with the demands of day-to-day modern life. It's time to move away from the idea that one's mental health is the by-product of a single neurotransmitter or protein. Each and every one of us has the power to heal our brains through simple lifestyle changes. We can embrace the knowledge, patterns, habits, and skills to help us build a more enjoyable, more mentally sound life.

Once you start moving away from the idea that your mental health can be managed through modulating a single neurotransmitter or gene, you'll start to understand just how much control you have over the health of your own brain. And because Mental Fitness is not a result, but a journey, you can always adapt how you implement the different lifestyle changes. You can do what works best for you. In doing so, you help put your brain in a perpetual state of self-repair and evolution.

Self-awareness. Nutrition. Movement. Sleep. Connection. Engagement. Grounding. Unburdening. Purpose. Each of these essential aspects of brain health has the power to make tremendous changes to your mental health and well-being. When you put them all together, that power grows exponentially. When we can optimize our Mental Fitness, we can better promote neurogenesis, dampen inflammation, and up the diversity in our microbiomes. We can give our brains the resources they need to thrive, even in the midst of all the stressors found in the modern world.

When you look around, it's clear that we need Mental Fitness more than ever. It will allow us to lean into the world as it is—and as it continues to evolve in ways we cannot even begin to fathom—to meet it with healthy and engaged brains. The good news is that we can embrace these core tenets to give the gift of Mental Fitness to ourselves and the people we love. We can use these skills to face the modern world with grace, healing, and steadiness, no matter what it throws our way.

This revolution begins, right here, right now, with you.

Acknowledgments

As AI was introduced and I learned about how large language models (LLMs) were trained, I thought that the mind of a psychiatrist is pretty similar. I've been trained by listening to patients and their families for twenty-five years as a physician focused on mental health concerns. Word by word, session by session, over the weeks and years, I've done my best to help heal the modern brains that sought my help, learning more each time. My first acknowledgment is to my patients, past and present, to whom I dedicate this book. Thank you for everything that you have shared with me.

I turned fifty writing this book. And perhaps more than any time in my life, I've needed these tenets of Mental Fitness. My family and I moved from the verdant pastures of the Indiana farm, found throughout this book, to the high mountains of western Wyoming. Transitions are filled with mental health challenges, and this one came with negative-twenty-degree weather and seven hundred inches of snow each winter.

Thank you to the members of my team. I'm so grateful to you all. Thank you, Alex Kariotis, for managing the internal operations and communications, allowing me to do more than I ever imagined. Thank you, Samantha Elkrief, for being you and taking care of brand, team, and the flame of associative process. I am very blessed to have the artist Jennie West as our finance director to trust with the money and creative flow. Thank you, Andrew Luer, for your drive and challenge to reach more people and change more lives. We're getting there. Thanks for being so blunt and personal at the same time.

My clinical team at the Brain Food Clinic and Spruce Mental Health have added to my life and practice what so many therapists miss: community and group process. Thanks, Xiaojue Hu, MD, for your steadiness, smarts, and growth mindset. Thank you, Emilie Berner, for the Mental Fitness Kitchen (sign up!) and the most delicious, nutrient-dense recipes one could hope for. Thank you to my team at Spruce Mental Health: Ben Smoak, MD; Tanmeet Sethi, MD; Jeff Greenbaum, MD; Amy Lane; and Margaret Brigham, for all of your perspectives and encouragement.

Thank you, Karen Rinaldi, for believing in me and these ideas. We've published five books together, and that is one of the most incredible honors of my life. Thank you to my literary agent, Joy Tutela, and her team at the David Black Literary Agency, for being loyal and decisive. Thank you, Kayt Sukel. Writing, working, and editing with you has been steady and dependable during a time of upheaval for me. You are a pretty good amateur therapist, too.

Over the last fifteen years publishing books and creating content, I've been fortunate that editors and producers at top media outlets have shared opportunities and feedback. Thank you to Rich Dorment, Marty Munson, Ben Court, Sean Abrams, and the great team at *Men's Health* magazine. Thank you, Jason and Colleen Wacob, Melisse Gelula, and the team at WebMD/Medscape. Thank you to the many podcasters who have hosted me and promoted the ideas of nutritional psychiatry and Mental Fitness.

Thank you to my psychiatry family. I regularly get to interview or collaborate with some of the finest minds in mental health. Today, some of my peers are leading academic departments and major research initiatives that will change how we understand mental health. I think about you all quite often, wondering what you think about a subject or how your brilliant mind sees a modern neural network or the epigenetics of BDNF or how shaking and dancing might help people with trauma. Thank you to the many members, past and present, of the Columbia University Department of Psychiatry who have mentored me and helped me over the years; Jim Gordon, MD, and the Center for Mind-Body Medicine; Nellie Hudson and the Bring Change 2 Mind team; and my many friends and colleagues at the American Psychiatric Association. Thank you to the many researchers and clinicians focused on mental health and nutritional psychiatry, particularly Felice Jacka, PhD, and her team at the Food and Mood Center. Thank you to all my mental health brothers and sisters in the media: Gregory Scott Brown, MD; Sue Varma, MD; Jake Goodman, MD; Sasha Hamdani, MD; David Puder, MD; Jessi Gold, MD; and Ally Jaffee, MD; to name a few of the many creative psychiatrists who keep the mental health social media conversation healthy and inspiring. Lastly, thank you to my colleagues focused on the impact of food on brain health and mental health: Annie Fenn, MD; Uma Naidoo, MD; Shebani Sethi, MD; Emily Deans, MD; and Laura LaChance, MD.

Since my last book was published, a few friends who have inspired and encouraged me have passed away. I found they were on my mind while working on this, especially during the harder times. Thank you, David Bouley, for celebrating food and health and showing us the power of connection. Thank you, Bret Stetka. Thank you, Cinco, for the big jumps.

Thank you. I'm sure that in some way, large or small, your interest in mental health and Mental Fitness contributed to making this book a reality. If you've ever bought one of my other books, liked or shared a social media post, signed up for our emails, left a comment, sent a DM, or listened to a podcast, it meant something to me and helped get this book in your hands.

Thank you, Tetons. This book was written in our new community in Jackson, Wyoming, a place of rugged natural beauty that is also a very intentional community interested in fitness and mental health. Thank you, Dr. Lux, Jerret, Emmet, and Hannah for all the adventures. I'd be a serious Mental Fitness hypocrite without you. Thank you, Peta, Gary, and the Roubin family for all of your kindness and even a pasture. Thank you, Burns, Floyd, Obleness, Hunt, Souter, Temple, Troxel, Hayashida-Ludington, and the many families who now touch our lives. What fun to be on this ride with you all. Thank you, Sarah, Emma, and the TYFS family.

Thank you to my parents for your encouragement. Thanks, Dad, for being a sharp-eyed copy editor. Thank you, Mom, for teaching me to grow and cook food. Thanks to my wonderful brother, Don; his wife, Corrine; and our nieces Penny, Odile, and Satie. The best is yet to come for us. Thank you, Ian McSpadden, for forty-five years of friendship, photos, big drops, and the sauna.

Thank you to my wife, Lucy, for all your good sense and commitment to mental health, especially mine. You are making good progress. Coffee service forever and ever, amen. Thank you, Greta, for being so thoughtful, fun, and responsible (cue teen side-eye); and Forrest, for making us popular, knowing facts, and caring about the details. Thank you, Juno, Bernadoodle Noodle, for the emotional support. Let's ditch these screens and head into the mountains.

Notes

INTRODUCTION

xiv   **I wasn't surprised that their findings**: J. Moncrieff et al., "The Serotonin Theory of Depression: A Systematic Umbrella Review of the Evidence," *Molecular Psychiatry* (2022), https://doi.org/10.1038/s41380-022-01661-0.

xv   **And a shocking number of people**: Mental Health America, "The State of Mental Health in America," 2022, https://mhanational.org/issues/state-mental-health-america.

xvi   **We've lived through a cruel pandemic**: World Health Organization, "The Impact of COVID-19 on Mental Health Cannot Be Made Light Of," June 16, 2022, https://www.who.int/news-room/feature-stories/detail/the-impact-of-covid-19-on-mental-health-cannot-be-made-light-of.

CHAPTER 3: SELF-AWARENESS

33   **Being able to see ourselves clearly**: T. Eurich, "What Self-Awareness Really Is (and How to Cultivate It)," *Harvard Business Review*, January 4, 2018, https://membership.amavic.com.au/files/What%20self-awareness%20is%20and%20how%20to%20cultivate%20it_HBR_2018.pdf.

39   **He also hypothesizes**: J. Haiteng et al., "Brain-Heart Interactions Underlying Traditional Tibetan Buddhist Meditation," *Cerebral Cortex* 30, no. 2 (2020): 439–50.

41   **The researchers found that breathwork**: M. Y. Balban et al., "Brief Structured Respiration Practices Enhance Mood and Reduce

Physiological Arousal," *Cell Reports Medicine* 4, no. 1 (2023): 100895.

CHAPTER 4: NUTRITION

50   **Many of us have been warned:** J. Ducharme, Almost 40% of Americans Eat Fast Food on Any Given Day, Report Says," *Time*, October 3, 2018, https://time.com/5412796/fast-food-americans/.

50   **Numerous studies have shown:** "Acrylamide and Cancer Risk," National Cancer Institute, accessed September 1, 2023, https://www.cancer.gov/about-cancer/causes-prevention/risk/diet/acrylamide-fact-sheet; B. Wang et al., "Acrylamide Exposure Increases Cardiovascular Risk of General Adult Population Probably by Inducing Oxidative Stress, Inflammation, and TGFβ1: A Prospective Cohort Study," *Environmental International* (June 2022): 164, https://doi.org/10.1016/j.envint.2022.107261.

50   **The researchers exposed zebrafish:** A. Wang et al., "High Fried Food Consumption Impacts Anxiety and Depression Due to Lipid Metabolism Disturbance and Neuroinflammation," *PNAS* 120, no. 18 (2023), https://doi.org/10.1073/pnas.2221097120.

51   **In fact, when researchers:** C. Samuthpongtorn et al., "Consumption of Ultraprocessed Food and Risk of Depression," *JAMA Network Open* 6, no. 9 (2023): e2334770, https://jamanetwork.com/journals/jamanetworkopen/fullarticle/2809727.

51   **Even after controlling for factors:** M. M. Lane et al., "High Ultra-Processed Food Consumption Is Associated with Elevated Psychological Distress as an Indicator of Depression in Adults from the Melbourne Collaborative Cohort Study," *Journal of Affective Disorders* 335 (2023): 57–66, https://pubmed.ncbi.nlm.nih.gov/37149054/.

52   **According to the Rudd Center for Food Policy:** J. L. Harris et al., "Food Advertising to Children and Teens (FACTS) Report," UConn Rudd Center for Food Policy & Obesity, 2021, https://media.ruddcenter.uconn.edu/PDFs/FACTS2021.pdf.

52   **Kids who spend their time:** F. Fleming-Milici, L. Phaneuf, and J. Harris, "Prevalence of Food and Beverage Brands in 'Made-for-Kids' Child-Influencer YouTube Videos: 2019–2020," *Pediatric Obesity* 18, no. 4 (2023): e13008, https://doi.org/10.1111/ijpo.13008; F. Fleming-Milici and J. L. Harris, "Adolescents' Engagement with Unhealthy Food and Beverage Brands on Social Media," *Appetite* (2020): 146.

57   **To understand which nutrients:** L. R. LaChance and D. Ramsey, "Antidepressant Foods: An Evidence-Based Nutrient Profiling System for Depression," *World Journal of Psychiatry* 8, no. 3 (2018): 97–104.

62   **And it lowers your risk:** A. Ventriglio et al., "Mediterranean Diet and Its Benefits on Health and Mental Health: A Literature Review," *Clinical Practice and Epidemiology in Mental Health* 16, Suppl. 1 (2020): 156–64.

62   **For example, Jacka demonstrated:** F. N. Jacka et al., "A Randomized Controlled Trial of Dietary Improvement for Adults with Major Depression (the 'SMILES' Trial)," *BMC Medicine* 15 (2017), https://doi.org/10.1186/s12916-017-0791-y.

62   **After twelve weeks:** J Bayes et al., "The Effect of a Mediterranean Diet on the Symptoms of Depression in Young Males (the 'AMMEND: A Mediterranean Diet in MEN with Depression' Study): A Randomized Controlled Trial," *American Journal of Clinical Nutrition* 116, no. 2 (2022): 572–80.

65   **The fewer ultraprocessed foods:** M. M. Lane et al., "Change in Ultra-Processed Food Consumption Moderates Clinical Trial Outcomes in Depression: A Secondary Analysis of the SMILES Randomized Controlled Trial," Preprints.org, 2023, https://www.preprints.org/manuscript/202308.1110/v1.

68   **A 2024 pilot study:** S. Sethi et al., "Ketogenic Diet Intervention on Metabolic and Psychiatric Health in Bipolar and Schizophrenia: A Pilot Trial," *Psychiatry Research* 335 (2024): 115866, https://www.sciencedirect.com/science/article/pii/S0165178124001513?via%3Dihub.

CHAPTER 5: MOVEMENT

76   **According to the National Institutes of Health:** E. Y. Duffy et al., "Opportunities to Improve Cardiovascular Health in the New American Workplace," *American Journal of Preventive Cardiology* 5 (March 2021), https://doi.org/10.1016/j.ajpc.2020.100136.

78   **He and his colleagues aimed:** H. van Praag, G. Kempermann, and F. H. Gage, "Running Increases Cell Proliferation and Neurogenesis in the Adult Mouse Dentate Gyrus," *Nature Neuroscience* 2, no. 3 (1999): 266–70.

79   **Studies have shown:** R. E. Ross et al., "The Role of Exercise in the Treatment of Depression: Biological Underpinnings and Clinical Outcomes," *Molecular Psychiatry* 28, no. 1 (2023): 298–328.

79   **they also talk to other organs:** M. Rai and F. Demontis, "Muscle-to-Brain Signaling via Myokines and Myometabolites," *Brain Plasticity* 8 (2022): 43–63; J. H. Bae and W. Song, "Brain and Brawn: Role of Exercise-Induced Myokines," *Journal of Obesity and Metabolic Syndrome* 28, no. 3 (2019): 145–47.

80   **When the researchers followed up:** B. M. Hoffman et al., "Exercise and Pharmacotherapy in Patients with Major Depression: One-Year Follow-up of the SMILE Study," *Psychosomatic Medicine* 73, no. 2 (2011): 127–33.

80   **Years later, when Blumenthal:** J. A. Blumenthal et al., "The Role of Comorbid Anxiety in Exercise and Depression Trials: Secondary Analysis of the SMILE-II Randomized Clinical Trial," *Depression and Anxiety* (August 2020), https://doi.org/10.1002/da.23088.

80   **In a 2022 study:** G. Tikac, A. Unal, and F. Altug, "Regular Exercise Improves the Levels of Self-Efficacy, Self-Esteem and Body Awareness of Young Adults," *Journal of Sports Medicine and Physical Fitness* 62, no. 1 (2022): 157–61.

81   **The authors simply concluded:** K. W. Choi et al., "Assessment of Bidirectional Relationships Between Physical Activity and Depression Among Adults: A 2-Sample Mendelian Randomization Study," *JAMA Psychiatry* 76, no. 4 (2019): 399–408.

81   **Those studies also showed:** P. A. Adlard et al., "Voluntary Exercise Decrease Amyloid Load in a Transgenic Model of Alzheimer's Disease," *Journal of Neuroscience* 25, no. 17 (2005): 4217–21; A. Ionescu-Tucker et al., "Exercise Reduces H3K9me3 and Regulates Brain Derived Neurotrophic Factor and GABRA2 in an Age Dependent Manner," *Frontiers in Aging Neuroscience* 13 (2021): 798297.

82   **But they also added:** J. Gomes-Osman et al., "Exercise for Cognitive Brain Health in Aging," *Neurology: Clinical Practice* 8, no. 3 (2018): 257–65.

82   **A more recent meta-analysis:** M. Noetel et al., "Effect of Exercise for Depression: Systematic Review and Network Meta-Analysis of Randomized Controlled Trials," *BMJ* (2024): 384, https://www.bmj.com/content/384/bmj-2023-075847.

83   **They argue that dance:** A. Fong Yan et al., "The Effectiveness of Dance Interventions on Psychological and Cognitive Health Outcomes Compared with Other Forms of Physical Activity: A Systematic Review with Meta-Analysis," *Sports Medicine* 54 (2024): 1179–1205, https://doi.org/10.1007/s40279-023-01990-2.

85   **They discovered that study participants:** C.-L. Hung et al., "Effect of

Acute Exercise Mode on Serum Brain-Derived Neurotrophic Factor (BDNF) and Task Switching Performance," *Journal of Clinical Medicine* 7, no. 10 (2018), https://doi.org/10.3390%2Fjcm7100301.

85 **The pool of options:** B. Wipfli et al., "An Examination of Serotonin and Psychological Variables in the Relationship Between Exercise and Mental Health," *Scandinavian Journal of Medicine & Science in Sports* 21, no. 3 (2011): 474–81, https://doi.org/10.1111/j.1600 -0838.2009.01049.x; J. Montero-Marin et al., "Effectiveness of a Stretching Program on Anxiety Levels of Workers in a Logistic Platform: A Randomized Controlled Study," *Atencion Primaria* 45, no. 7 (2013): 376–83.

CHAPTER 6: SLEEP

90 **Tripp managed to achieve:** E. Inglis-Arkell, "The Sleep Deprivation Publicity Stunt That Drove One Man Crazy," Gizmodo, March 24, 2014, https://gizmodo.com/the-sleep-deprivation-publicity-stunt -that-drove-one-ma-1550084876.

94 **And this seemingly random recall:** B. Rasch and J. Born, "About Sleep's Role in Memory," *Physiological Reviews* 93, no. 2 (2013): 681–766, https://journals.physiology.org/doi/full/10.1152 /physrev.00032.2012.

94 **Those who went without it:** T.-M. Prince and T. Abel, "The Impact of Sleep Loss on Hippocampal Function," *Learning and Memory* 20, no. 10 (2013): 558–69, https://www.ncbi.nlm.nih.gov/pmc /articles/PMC3768199/.

95 **Researchers Giulio Tononi:** G. Tononi and C. Cirelli, "Sleep and the Price of Plasticity: From Synaptic and Cellular Homeostasis to Memory Consolidation and Integration," *Neuron* 81, no. 1 (2014): 12–34, https://www.cell.com/neuron/fulltext/S0896 -6273(13)01186-0.

98 **The researchers called it:** L. Xie et al., "Sleep Drives Metabolite Clearance from the Adult Brain," *Science* 342, no. 6156 (2013): 373–77, https://pubmed.ncbi.nlm.nih.gov/24136970/.

100 **The latest research:** Z. Wang et al., "Gut Microbiota Modulates the Inflammatory Response and Cognitive Impairment Induced by Sleep Deprivation," *Molecular Psychiatry* 26 (2021): 6277–92, https://www.nature.com/articles/s41380-021-01113-1.

103 **Sigmund Freud:** Sigmund Freud, *The Interpretation of Dreams* (Leipzig: Franz Deuticke, 1899).

103 **His theory:** A. Zadra and R. Stickgold, *When Brains Dream:*

Understanding the Science and Mystery of Our Dreaming Minds (New York: W. W. Norton & Company, 2021).

106 **A 2022 survey revealed:** A. Kerai, "Smart Phone Addiction Stats," Reviews.org, July 21, 2023, https://www.reviews.org/mobile/cell -phone-addiction/#Smart_Phone_Addiction_Stats.

CHAPTER 7: CONNECTION

112 **In 2023, he released:** US Department of Health and Human Services, "New Surgeon General Advisory Raises Alarm About the Devastating Impact of the Epidemic of Loneliness and Isolation in the United States," press release, May 3, 2023, https://www.hhs .gov/about/news/2023/05/03/new-surgeon-general-advisory-raises -alarm-about-devastating-impact-epidemic-loneliness-isolation -united-states.html.

115 **If you even still attend:** R. Steuteville, "The Missing Middle of Our Social Lives," *Public Square*, February 8, 2016, https://www.cnu .org/publicsquare/2016/02/08/missing-middle-our-social-lives.

116 **The downsides of social media:** Vivek H. Murthy, "Surgeon General: Why I'm Calling for a Warning Label on Social Media Platforms," *New York Times*, June 17, 2024, https://www.nytimes .com/2024/06/17/opinion/social-media-health-warning.html.

117 **A 2021 study of one million adolescents:** A. Levula, A. Wilson, and M. Harré, "The Association Between Social Network Factors and Mental Health at Different Life Stages," *Quality of Life Research* 25 (2015): 1725–33, https://link.springer.com/article/10.1007/s11136 -015-1200-7.

117 **Even adults who are avid social media users:** American Psychiatric Association, "New Survey Shows Increasing Loneliness, Including on the Job," February 10, 2020, https://www.psychiatry.org/news -room/apa-blogs/new-survey-shows-increasing-loneliness-on-the -job.

118 **While there is a lot we can do via computer screen:** L. Kroencke et al., "Well-Being in Social Interactions: Examining Personality-Situation Dynamics in Face-to-Face and Computer-Mediated Communication," *Journal of Personality and Social Psychology* 124, no. 2 (2023), 437–60, https://psycnet.apa.org/record/2022-80655-001?doi=1.

121 **The scientists found:** J. Holt-Lunstad, T. B. Smith, J. B. Layton, "Social Relationships and Mortality Risk: A Meta-Analytic Review," *PLOS Medicine* 7, no. 7 (2010): e1000316, https://journals.plos .org/plosmedicine/article?id=10.1371/journal.pmed.1000316.

121   **Having social support:** J. Salinas et al., "Associations Between Social Relationship Measures, Serum Brain-Derived Neurotrophic Factor, and Risk of Stroke and Dementia," *Alzheimer's and Dementia* 3, no. 2 (2017): 229–37, https://www.ncbi.nlm.nih.gov /pmc/articles/PMC5651441/.

121   **Other studies show:** C. Y. Yang, K. Schorpp, and K. M. Harris, "Social Support, Social Strain and Inflammation: Evidence from a National Longitudinal Study of U.S. Adults," *Social Science and Medicine* 107 (2014): 124–35, https://www.ncbi.nlm.nih.gov/pmc /articles/PMC4028709/.

123   **So perhaps it's not surprising:** H. K. Collins et al., "Relational Diversity in Social Portfolios Predicts Well-Being," *PNAS* 119, no. 43 (2022): e2120668119, https://www.pnas.org/doi /full/10.1073/pnas.2120668119.

126   **Or you can take:** U.S. Department of Health and Human Services, "Take the Surgeon General's 5-for-5 Connection Challenge," https://www.hhs.gov/surgeongeneral/priorities/connection /challenge/index.html.

128   **In 2019, Swiss researchers:** O. Hämmig, "Correction: Health Risks Associated with Social Isolation in General and in Young, Middle and Old Age," *PLOS ONE* 14, no. 8 (2019): e0222124, https://doi .org/10.1371/journal.pone.0222124.

CHAPTER 8: ENGAGEMENT

133   **This goes beyond:** K. Sukel, "Defying Dementia: It Is Not Inevitable," *New Scientist*, April 26, 2017, https://institutions .newscientist.com/article/mg23431230-400-defying-dementia-it-is -not-inevitable/.

133   **Many experts now suggest:** K. P. Muliyala and M. Varghese, "The Complex Relationship Between Depression and Dementia," *Annals of Indian Academy of Neurology* 13, Suppl. 2 (2010): S69–S73, https://www.ncbi.nlm.nih.gov/pmc/articles/PMC3039168/.

133   **Interestingly enough:** S. Hayley, A. M. Hakim, and P. R. Albert, "Depression, Dementia and Immune Dysregulation," *Brain* 144, no. 3 (2021): 746–60, https://www.ncbi.nlm.nih.gov/pmc/articles /PMC8041341/.

135   **While it would be all too easy:** D. Thompson, "It Sure Looks Like Phones Are Making Students Dumber," *Atlantic*, December 19, 2023, https://www.theatlantic.com/ideas/archive/2023/12/cell -phones-student-test-scores-dropping/676889/.

138   **so much so that:** National Health Service, "5 Steps to Mental
Wellbeing," December 16, 2022, https://www.nhs.uk/mental-health
/self-help/guides-tools-and-activities/five-steps-to-mental-wellbeing/.

138   **A study in a Japanese community:** M. Hirosaki et al., "Community-
Dwelling Elderly Japanese People with Hobbies Are Healthier than
Those Lacking Hobbies," *JAGS* 57, no. 6 (2009): 1132–33, https://
agsjournals.onlinelibrary.wiley.com/doi/pdf/10.1111/j.1532
-5415.2009.02291.x.

138   **Seventy-seven percent:** D. Fancourt, S. Opher, and C. de Oliveira,
"Fixed-Effects Analyses of Time-Varying Associations Between
Hobbies and Depression in a Longitudinal Cohort Study: Support
for Social Prescribing?" *Psychotherapy and Psychosomatics* 89 (2020):
111–13, https://karger.com/pps/article-pdf/89/2/111/3482634
/000503571.pdf.

139   **They had higher self-esteem:** C. Hammond, "Impacts of Lifelong
Learning upon Emotional Resilience, Psychological and Mental
Health: Fieldwork Evidence," *Oxford Review of Education* 30, no. 4
(2007): 551–68, https://www.tandfonline.com/doi/abs/10.1080
/03054980420003003008.

139   **What you are looking for:** R. T. Staff et al., "Intellectual
Engagement and Cognitive Ability in Later Life (the 'Use it or Lose
It' Conjecture): Longitudinal, Prospective Study," *BMJ* (2018),
https://doi.org/10.1136/bmj.k4925; J. Lavrijsen and K. Verschueren,
"High Cognitive Ability and Mental Health: Findings from a Large
Community Sample of Adolescents," *Journal of Intelligence* 11, no. 2
(2023): 38, https://www.ncbi.nlm.nih.gov/pmc/articles
/PMC9966861/.

140   **They hypothesized that one reason:** A. Fong Yan et al., "The
Effectiveness of Dance Interventions on Psychological and Cognitive
Health Outcomes Compared with Other Forms of Physical Activity:
A Systematic Review with Meta-Analysis," *Sports Medicine* 54
(2024): 1179–1205, https://doi.org/10.1007/s40279-023-01990-2.

141   **Cognitive engagement also has the benefit:** C. Pettigrew and
A. Soldan, "Defining Cognitive Reserve and Implications for
Cognitive Aging," *Current Neurology and Neuroscience Reports* 19,
no. 1 (2019), https://doi.org/10.1007/s11910-019-0917-z.

CHAPTER 9: GROUNDING

148   **The United Nations expects:** United Nations, "Make Cities and
Human Settlements Inclusive, Safe, Resilient, and Sustainable,"
2022, https://unstats.un.org/sdgs/report/2022/goal-11/.

148   **Projections for the United States:** University of Michigan Center for Sustainable Systems, "U.S. Cities Factsheet," https://css.umich .edu/publications/factsheets/built-environment/us-cities-factsheet.

149   **That's the sound equivalent:** K. Wagner, "City Noise Might Be Making You Sick," *Atlantic*, February 20, 2018, https://www .theatlantic.com/technology/archive/2018/02/city-noise-might-be -making-you-sick/553385/.

149   **And yes, they are:** M. Basner et al., "Auditory and Non-Auditory Effects of Noise on Health," *Lancet* 383, no. 9925 (2014): 1325–32, https://www.ncbi.nlm.nih.gov/pmc/articles/PMC3988259/.

149   **Indeed, the World Health Organization:** World Health Organization, "Europe: Noise," https://www.who.int/europe /health-topics/noise#tab=tab_1.

149   **Bright lights are the norm:** W. Gleason, "Check Out This Mind-Blowing Photo of NYC from Space," *Time Out*, February 29, 2016, https://www.timeout.com/newyork/blog/check-out-this-mind -blowing-photo-of-nyc-from-space-022916.

149   **A recent study of more than 85,000 people:** A. C. Burns et al., "Day and Night Light Exposure Are Associated with Psychiatric Disorders: An Objective Light Study in >85,000 People," *Nature Mental Health* 1 (2023): 853–62, https://www.nature.com/articles /s44220-023-00135-8.

150   **That extra light can knock:** J. J. Gooley et al., "Exposure to Room Light Before Bedtime Suppresses Melatonin Onset and Shortens Melatonin Duration in Humans," *Journal of Clinical Endocrinology and Metabolism* 96, no. 3 (2011): E463–72, https://doi.org/10.1210 /jc.2010-2098.

151   **As a result:** R. Jimison, "We All Need Green in Our Lives, CNN Health, June 5, 2017, https://www.cnn.com/2017/06/05/health /colorscope-green-environment-calm/index.html.

152   **These are special white blood cells:** Q. Li, "Effect of Forest Bathing Trips on Human Immune Function," *Environmental Health and Preventive Medicine* 15, no. 1 (2010): 9–17, https://www.ncbi.nlm .nih.gov/pmc/articles/PMC2793341/.

155   **Studies that compare the mental health:** Z. Liu et al., "Green Space Exposure on Depression and Anxiety Outcomes: A Meta-Analysis," *Environmental Research* 231, no. 3 (2023): 116303, https://www .sciencedirect.com/science/article/abs/pii/S0013935123011076.

155   **Other research suggests:** M. Rueff and G. Reese, "Depression and Anxiety: A Systematic Review on Comparing Ecotherapy with Cognitive Behavioral Therapy," *Journal of Environmental Psychology*

90 (2023): 102097, https://www.sciencedirect.com/science/article
/abs/pii/S0272494423001457.

155   **There are now dozens:** S. Dorfman, "Ecotherapy: How
Communing with Nature Boosts Your Physical and Mental
Health," *USA Today*, August 8, 2022, https://www.usatoday.com
/story/life/health-wellness/2022/08/08/ecotherapy-health-benefits
-nature/10264052002.

156   **When researchers played nature sounds:** M. Nasari, T. N.
Ghezeljeh, and H. Haghani, "Effects of Nature Sounds on Sleep
Quality Among Patients Hospitalized in Coronary Care Units:
A Randomized Controlled Clinical Trial," *Nursing and Midwifery
Studies* 7, no. 1 (2018): 18–23, https://journals.lww.com/nams
/Fulltext/2018/07010/Effects_of_Nature_Sounds_on_Sleep
_Quality_among.4.aspx.

157   **In addition:** S. Xiao et al., "Biological Effects of Negative Air
Ions on Human Health and Integrated Multiomics to Identify
Biomarkers: A Literature Review," *Environmental Science and
Pollution Research* 30, no. 27 (2023): 69824–36, https://www.ncbi
.nlm.nih.gov/pmc/articles/PMC10175061/.

157   **In fact, a 2015 study:** G. Chevalier, "The Effect of Grounding the
Human Body on Mood," *Psychological Reports* 116, no. 2 (2015),
https://doi.org/10.2466/06.PR0.116k21w5.

158   **Other studies have shown:** S. T. Sinatra et al., "Grounding: The
Universal Anti-Inflammatory Remedy," *Biomedical Journal* 46, no.
1 (2023): 11–16, https://www.ncbi.nlm.nih.gov/pmc/articles
/PMC10105021/.

158   **But with research studies showing:** C. Wesselman, "Green Spaces
and Human Health," Centers for Disease Control and Prevention,
September 8, 2022, https://storymaps.arcgis.com/stories
/a9dab1f292be48a89d18b433fa3cbba6.

158   **hospital invested in creating the Commonground:** Eskenazi
Health, "Eskenazi Health Celebrates Opening of World-Class
Outdoor Plaza," press release, July 29, 2014, https://www
.eskenazihealth.edu/news/eskenazi-health-celebrates-opening-of
-world-class-outdoor-plaza.

160   **It's merely the act:** S. Fitzgerald, "The Secret to Mindful Travel?
A Walk in the Woods," *National Geographic*, October 18, 2019,
https://www.nationalgeographic.com/travel/article/forest-bathing
-nature-walk-health.

160   **The deactivation in the amygdala:** S. Sudimac, V. Sale, and
S. Kuhn, "How Nature Nurtures: Amygdala Activity Decreases as

the Result of a One-Hour Walk in Nature," *Molecular Psychiatry* 27 (2022): 4446–52, https://www.nature.com/articles/s41380-022 -01720-6.

161   **It's why the American Psychological Association:** American Psychological Association, "Mental Health and Our Changing Climate: Impacts, Implications, and Guidance," March 2017, https://www.apa.org/news/press/releases/2017/03/mental-health -climate.pdf.

162   **When we understand:** D. Pollack and E. Haase, "What Every Psychiatrist Should Know About the Climate Crisis," *Psychiatric News* 57, no. 6 (2022), https://psychnews.psychiatryonline.org/doi /full/10.1176/appi.pn.2022.06.6.36.

CHAPTER 10: UNBURDENING

167   **To start, as noted by Canadian physician:** J. Nerenberg, "Why Are So Many Adults Today Haunted by Trauma?" *Greater Good*, June 8, 2017, https://greatergood.berkeley.edu/article/item/why_are_so _many_adults_today_haunted_by_trauma.

167   **Second, the United States:** Commonwealth Fund, "Understanding the U.S. Behavioral Health Workforce Shortage," May 18, 2023, https://www.commonwealthfund.org/publications/explainer/2023 /may/understanding-us-behavioral-health-workforce-shortage.

167   **Even the White House:** The White House, "Reducing the Economic Burden of Unmet Mental Health Needs," May 31, 2022, https://www.whitehouse.gov/cea/written-materials/2022/05/31 /reducing-the-economic-burden-of-unmet-mental-health-needs/.

169   **What's more, the more ACEs:** Centers for Disease Control and Prevention, "Adverse Childhood Experiences (ACEs)," August 23, 2021, https://www.cdc.gov/vitalsigns/aces/index.html.

171   **That is part of the basis of exposure:** D. M. Hezel and H. B. Simpson, "Exposure and Response Prevention for Obsessive-Compulsive Disorder: A Review and New Directions," *Indian Journal of Psychiatry* 61, Suppl. 1 (2019): S85–S92, https://journals .lww.com/indianjpsychiatry/fulltext/2019/61001/exposure_and _response_prevention_for.12.aspx.

CHAPTER 11: PURPOSE

176   **This, the authors suggested:** K. Shiba et al., "Purpose in Life and 8-Year Mortality by Gender and Race/Ethnicity Among Older Adults in the U.S.," *Preventive Medicine* 164 (2022): 107310,

https://www.sciencedirect.com/science/article/abs/pii
/S0091743522003590.

176   **Across a wide range of studies:** I. D. Boreham and N. S. Schutte,
"The Relationship Between Purpose in Life and Depression and
Anxiety: A Meta-Analysis," *Journal of Clinical Psychology* 79, no.
12(2023): 2736–67, https://doi.org/10.1002/jclp.23576.

176   **They also show healthier activity:** A. K. Nair et al., "Purpose in Life
as a Resilience Factor for Brain Health: Diffusion MRI Findings
from the Midlife in the U.S. Study," *Frontiers in Psychiatry* 15
(2024), https://doi.org/10.3389/fpsyt.2024.1355998.

176   **Still other studies:** K. Abellaneda-Pérez et al., "Purpose in Life
Promotes Resilience to Age-Related Brain Burden in Middle-Aged
Adults," *Alzheimer's Research and Therapy* 15, no. 1 (2023): 49,
https://pubmed.ncbi.nlm.nih.gov/36915148/.

177   **Even on stressful days:** P. L. Hill et al., "Sense of Purpose
Moderates the Associations Between Daily Stressors and Daily
Well-Being," *Annals of Behavioral Medicine* 52, no. 8 (2018):
724–29, https://academic.oup.com/abm/article/52/8/724/4841716.

177   **Other studies have shown:** K. C. Bronk, S. Leontopoulou, and
J. McConchie, "Youth Purpose During the Great Recession: A
Mixed-Methods Study," *Journal of Positive Psychology* 14, no. 4
(2019): 405–16, https://www.tandfonline.com/doi/pdf/10.1080
/17439760.2018.1484942.

CONCLUSION: BUILDING A MORE RESILIENT BRAIN

185   **With all the buzz about psychedelics:** A. Jacobs, "The Psychedelic
Revolution Is Coming: Psychiatry May Never Be the Same," *New
York Times,* May 9, 2021, https://www.nytimes.com/2021/05/09
/health/psychedelics-mdma-psilocybin-molly-mental-health.html.

186   **Today, the latest psychopharmacology research:** J. Davidson,
"VA Considers Using Psychedelic Drugs to Fight PTSD Among
Veterans," *Washington Post,* February 16, 2024, https://www
.washingtonpost.com/politics/2024/02/16/va-psychedelics-mdma
-psilocybin-ptsd/.

186   **Studies show that compounds:** C. M. Reiff et al., "Psychedelics
and Psychedelic-Assisted Psychotherapy," *American Journal of
Psychiatry* 177, no. 5 (2020): 391–410, https://pubmed.ncbi.nlm
.nih.gov/32098487/.

186   **In a 2021 randomized clinical trial:** A. K. Davis et al., "Effects of
Psilocybin-Assisted Therapy on Major Depressive Disorder: A

Randomized Clinical Trial," *JAMA Psychiatry* 78, no. 5 (2021): 481–89, https://pubmed.ncbi.nlm.nih.gov/33146667/.

186   **They also explain the main side effects:** R. Carhart-Harris, "How Do Psychedelics Work?" *Current Opinion in Psychiatry* 32, no. 1 (2019): 16–21, https://pubmed.ncbi.nlm.nih.gov/30394903/.

Index

About the Author

DREW RAMSEY, MD, is a board-certified psychiatrist, a psychotherapist, and an author. His work focuses on evidence-based integrative psychiatry treatments, psychodynamic psychotherapy, nutritional psychiatry, and responsible medication management. Using the latest mental health research and years of clinical experience, he hopes to help people improve their mental health and build resilient Mental Fitness.

He founded the Brain Food Clinic in New York City and Spruce Mental Health in Jackson, Wyoming. He served as an assistant clinical professor of psychiatry for twenty years at Columbia University, Vagelos College of Physicians and Surgeons, where he taught and supervised Psychiatric Evaluation, Supportive Psychotherapy, Brief Dynamic Psychotherapy, and Nutritional Psychiatry, as well as helping direct the department's media and social media initiatives.

Dr. Ramsey is a mental health advocate and influencer, and a compelling keynote speaker, and he conducts workshops nationally. He cohosts the *Men's Health* magazine series Friday Sessions with Gregory Scott Brown, MD, and has delivered three TEDx talks, a video series with Big Think, and the BBC documentary *Food on the Brain*. His work and writing have been featured by *The Today Show*, *CBS Sunday Morning*, the *New York Times*, the *Wall Street Journal*, *The Atlantic*, *Lancet Psychiatry*, *Time*, and NPR. He is on the editorial board of Medscape Psychiatry, the advisory board of *Men's Health*, and the scientific advisory board of the anti-stigma nonprofit Bring Change to Mind. He served as the chairman of the council for communications for the American Psychiatric Association.

He is the author of four books concerning food and mental health, most recently the international bestseller *Eat to Beat Depression and Anxiety*, now translated into nine languages; the award-winning cookbook *Eat Complete: The 21 Nutrients That Fuel Brainpower, Boost Weight Loss, and Transform Your Health*; the bestseller *Fifty Shades of Kale*; and *The Happiness Diet: A Nutritional Prescription for a Sharp Brain, Balanced Mood, and Lean, Energized Body*, which explores the impact of modern diets on brain health.

He and his team have created three e-courses: Healing the Modern Brain, Eat to Beat Depression, and Nutritional Psychiatry for Clinicians; along with free downloads, the *Mental Fitness Kitchen*, and the *Dr. Drew Ramsey Podcast*.

Dr. Ramsey is a diplomate of the American Board of Psychiatry and Neurology and a fellow of the American Psychiatric Association. He completed his specialty training in adult psychiatry at Columbia University and the New York State Psychiatric Institute, received an MD from Indiana University School of Medicine, and is a Phi Beta Kappa graduate of Earlham College. He lives in Jackson, Wyoming, with his wife and two children.

Learn more at DrewRamseyMD.com.